THE NAKED TRUTH

First published in 1967
This edition published in 2017

Wolfbait Books
157 Mornington Road, Leytonstone, London E11 3DT
www.wolfbait.co.uk

All images in this book have been reproduced with the knowledge and prior consent of the George Harrison Marks Enterprises Ltd, Peter B. Fairbrass and Yahya El-Droubie. Nine Ages of Nakedness photographer: Peter B. Fairbrass.

The publisher would like the thank the following people, who provided images and/or editorial assistance, without whose help this book would not have been possible: Yahya El-Droubie, Peter Fairbrass, Suzy Prince and Gavin Whitaker.

A CIP record for this book is available from the British Library
ISBN: 978-1-9997441-0-6 (paperback)
ISBN: 978-1-9997441-2-0 (ebook)

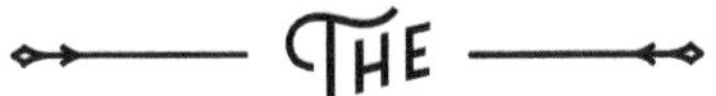

THE NAKED TRUTH

ABOUT HARRISON MARKS

FRANKLYN WOOD

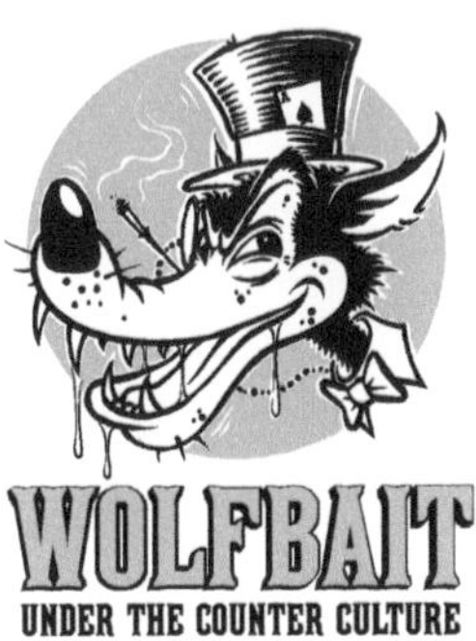

Acknowledgements are made to
Mr. Noel Botham for his assistance in research

ABOUT THE AUTHOR

JOURNALIST and author Franklyn Wood (1925 - 1991) was a former Art Editor of *The Times* and was the first editor in Fleet Street to run a diary (in *The Daily Sketch*) under his own name. He wrote numerous features in *The Sunday Times*, *News of the World* and other popular Sunday newspapers, women's magazines and continental journals on a variety of subjects ranging from shock, horror and scandal exposés, to business news.

Contents

Foreword

WHEN this book first appeared in 1967, public interest in glamour photographer and magazine publisher George Harrison Marks was arguably at an all-time high. Just who was this man with the beatnik beard, the thick frame glasses and the seemingly dream job of photographing beautiful women in a state of undress? A job that had made him the object of public idolisation, envy, curiosity and condemnation in equal proportions. Unravelling the Marks mystique was something the press had been attempting to do ever since Marks first made a name for himself with his nudie magazine *Kamera* in 1957, and Marks along with his muse/chief model/business partner Pamela Green had rarely been out of the public eye since then. Not that Harrison Marks was exactly the publicity-shy type. On the contrary, this was a man who clearly loved the limelight, a limelight he'd first gotten a taste for as a star-struck youngster in awe of the music hall greats whose antics provided some much-needed laughs and cheers during the war years that Marks grew up in.

As to how much naked truth made it into the 1960s biography of him that you now hold in your hands...hmm, I can't help thinking of the words of an associate of his who once told me that it would probably take a decade for someone to sort the truth about Marks' life from fanciful myths and tall tales he made up about himself over the years. More than a decade later I'm still trying to separate the naked truth from the bare faced lies Marks tells about himself in this book. Whatever the case though there can be no doubt that Marks was a born raconteur. This is a great book that grabs you by the lapels and drags you back into Britain's colourful past whilst telling the story of a nice Jewish boy who attempted to follow in his music hall idols footsteps by forming a comedy double act which toured the crumbling, fag end of the music hall era, and somehow ended up photographing nude women in the dark, violent, Bohemian world of 1950s Soho, before fame and fortune finally came a knocking in the 1960s.

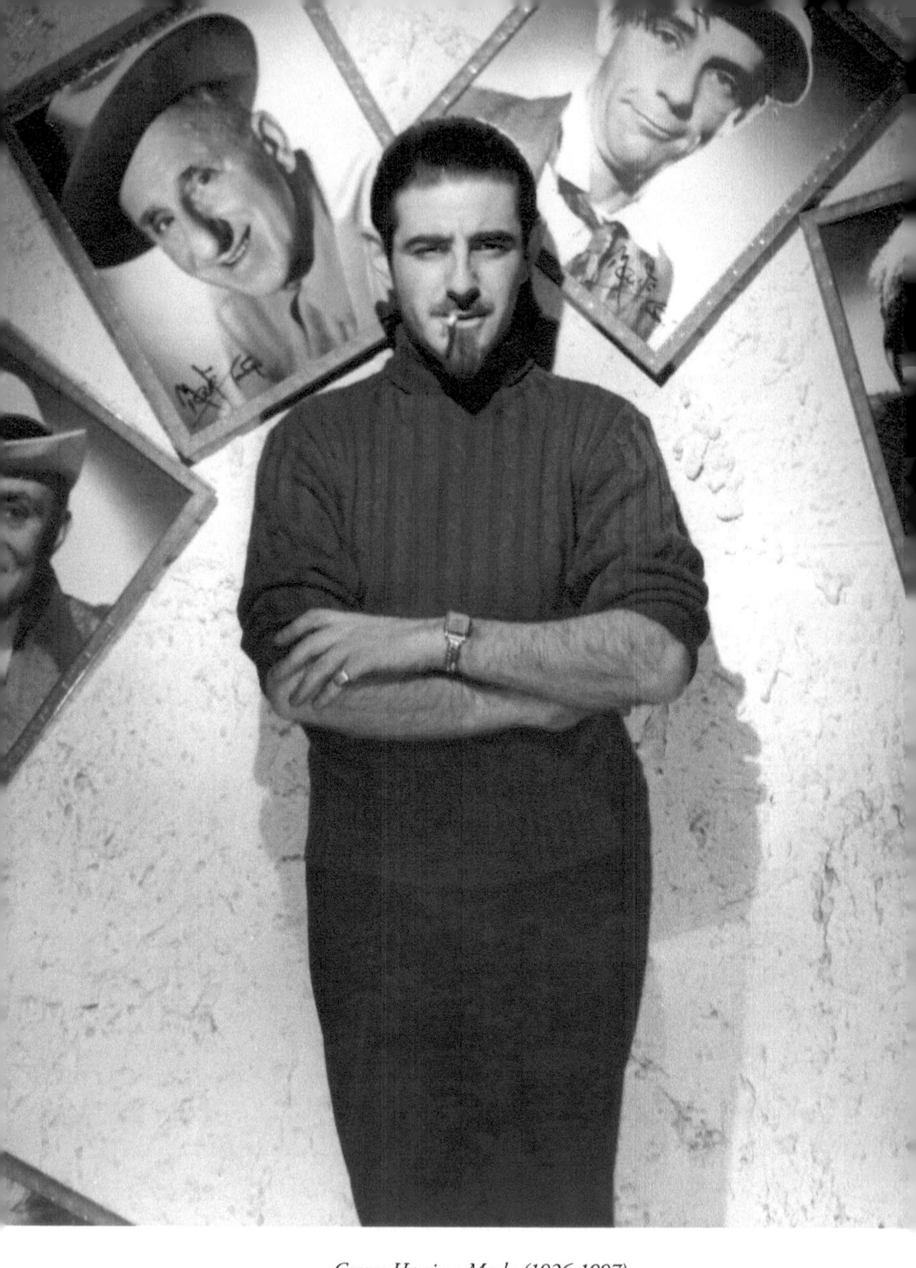

George Harrison Marks (1926-1997)

Girlfriends and wives may have come and gone over the years, but the music hall remained the great love of Marks' life. By all accounts, he possessed an encyclopaedic knowledge of music hall history (as can frequently be detected in this book itself) and its influence became an essential part of his personal shtick. Many of his rivals in the glamour photography game preferred to remain as anonymous as possible, but Marks' name, face and personality were all over *Kamera* from the get-go. A move into filmmaking offered a further chance for Marks to play the role of the eternal ham. 8mm glamour films like *The Window Dresser* (1961), and big screen outings *The Naked World of Harrison Marks* (1967) and *The Nine Ages of Nakedness* (1969), inevitably find their maker prancing around on screen, usually dressed up in some ridiculous disguise like the music hall star he never was. Films like those fulfilled Marks' showbiz aspirations, whilst making good on their pact with the lustful public by the delivering the expected parade of female breasts, bums and thighs that the Harrison Marks name had become synonymous with. Ask people about the man himself, and you're left with the impression of a true one off, and a life fully lived. Marks drank, womanised, smoked, swore, laughed, entertained friends, titillated the masses, saw his name in lights and saw his name dragged through the courts. "I've had a great time, I've made a fortune, and I've fucked a thousand beautiful women, what have I got to complain about" he claimed in 1985, and who could argue with that?

This book closes in 1967, with only a slight hint of the dark clouds that were gathering on the horizon. Marks would go bankrupt in 1969, and spent much of the next decade in the pornographic wilderness, filming smut of both the soft and hard varieties for men he'd come to despise. Some of the short porno films that emerged from that era surprisingly find Marks throwing all his creativity at them. They remain as distinctly Marksian creations as anything he put his name to (from Marks lesser documented 'blue period' I'd particularly recommend the lunacy of *Die Lollos, Autograph Hour, Dolly Mixture,* and *The Happy Nurses*). Sadly other chunks of his 1970s output remain mirthless, by the numbers, blue movies clearly just crapped out to keep the great man financially afloat.

1977 brought with it one final moment of big screen glory and saw Marks stepping out as director, writer and star of *Come Play With Me,* surely Marks' magnum opus and the ultimate example of his 'music hall meets pornography under the influence of a bottle of whisky' aesthetic. A film only Marks could or would want to make, *Come Play With Me* saw Marks and Alfie Bass play a pair of decrepit banknote forgers, whose attempts to hide out from East End gangsters at a health farm are thwarted by the arrival of a coachload of nympho nurses. Even the film's producer, David Sullivan, would later admit that Marks was "in a bit of a time warp…he thought he was making some vaudeville comedy, I thought it was a weird old film", and he isn't wrong. *Come Play With Me* is a film that will never be accused of being in touch with the times it was made in. While the disenchanted youth of 1977 were pogoing to the Sex Pistols' 'Anarchy in the U.K', *Come Play With Me* serves up the sight of Marks, Bass and the nurses performing the musical sing-along number 'It's Great to be Here' (all together now "it great to be here, there never ever could be anywhere else for me, this is where we want to be, here enjoying ourselves"). The British public, however, took *Come Play With Me* to its collective bosom, and the film went on the become an unlikely success story, one that played at the Cameo Moulin cinema in the West End for a record-breaking four-year run. A feat which continues to baffle the shit out of historians, cinema snobs and even some of the people who appeared in the film to this very day.

Marks finally left hardcore pornography behind him in 1979, then embarked on one final career reinvention as the publisher of *Kane*, a fine periodical dedicated to spanking in general, and corporal punishment in particular. *Kane* and other derriere whacking ventures, which included live spanking shows with Marks as MC and self-explanatory videos like *Schoolgirl Fannies on Fire* and *A Whacking in a Winter Wonderland*, may not have restored Marks to the wealth he had enjoyed in the 1960s, but kept him in 'modest luxury' until decades of smoking like a chimney, drinking like a fish and behaving like a rabbit finally caught up with him in June 1997. Marks' self-penned funeral programme included the strict instructions for his mourners to "get drunk…I want 'em all to get pissed, and I'll join 'em in spirit, as f***in' usual, and make sure they buy their own f***in' drinks".

I wish Marks were better remembered these days, anecdotes about the man himself never fail to entertain, and who else could claim to have had a career that spans music hall, glamour photography, pornography and the spanking industry. C'mon the man should be regarded as a national treasure, but maybe we're doing a tiny bit to right that wrong by reprinting this book, which has been out of print for several decades. So let's waste no more time in blowing the dust off the past and raising a glass (or several) to The Great Marko as he emerges from a cloud of his cigarette smoke and once again gets to be the centre of attention by delivering the "is it or isn't it" Naked Truth about his incredible, jam-packed life. I'm sure you'll agree that "It's Great to be Here".

Gavin Whitaker

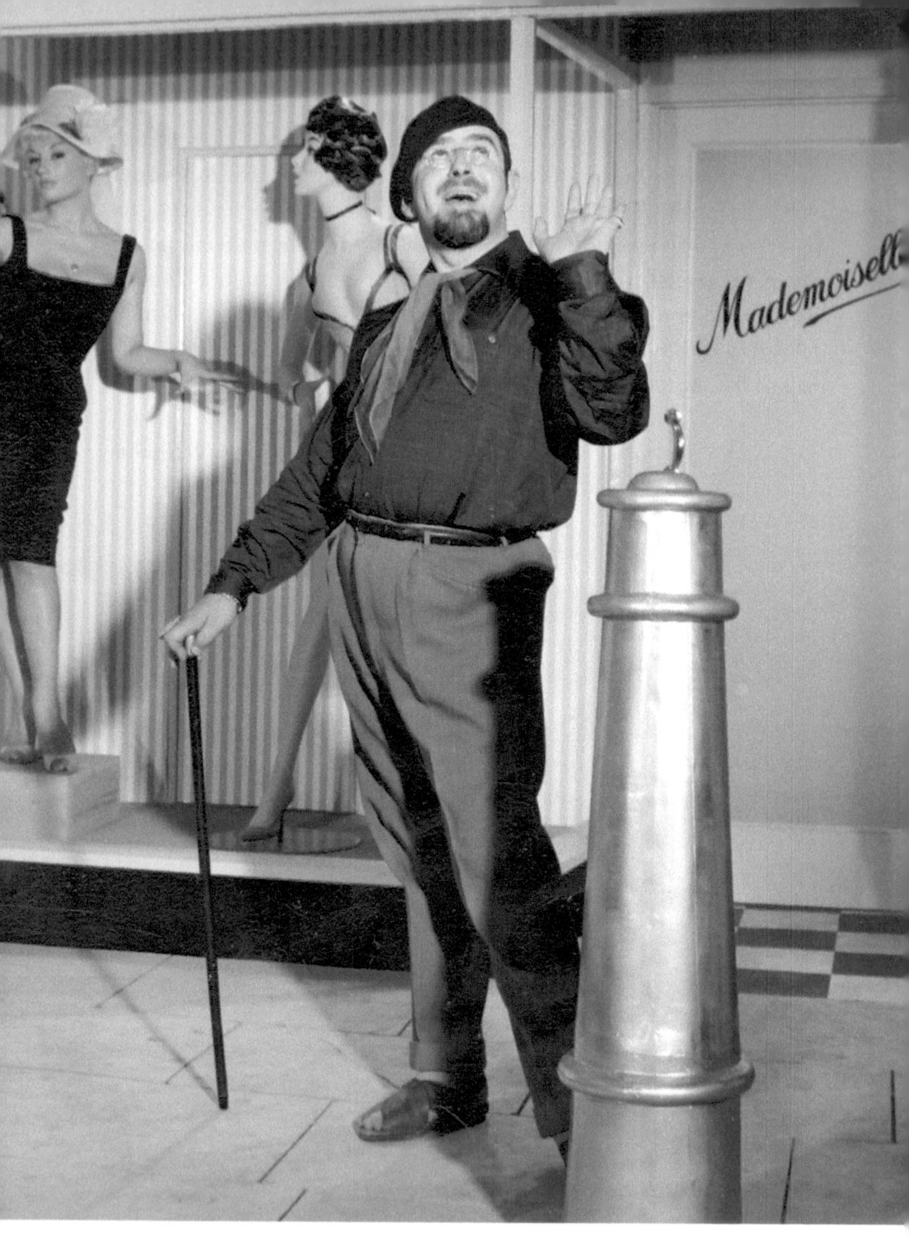

George Harrison Marks on the set of 'The Window Dresser', with Pamela Green, posing as a mannequin, in the background

Introduction

READING through the proofs of this book, I have asked myself why I have allowed these series of happenings in my life to be published. Suddenly here is a book… it certainly didn't start out as such. Then how did it start?

A group of friends sitting around, drinking and talking of their past experiences, both amorous and personal. And somebody saying, "Christ, that would make interesting reading.

Has my life up to now been interesting? I don't honestly know. I do know that in spite of the ups and downs scattered through it, I've enjoyed it. Reading through the following pages, I've wondered whether my experiences have been any zippier than most other people experiences. I admit that I may have had more than my share of some of the better pleasures of life, it possibly reads so. But then it's all condensed here into a couple of hundred pages, and, let's face it, it has taken me more than 3,650 days — and nights — to live it. It doesn't seem so hectic when you put it that way, does it?

Even as I've renewed the memories of my encounters with life on reading this book, still more edge their way in — like spending a wonderful week alone with a Countess at her Château in the Black Forest. How I found myself browsing through one of the world's largest and most expensive collections of pornography owned by one of France's greatest actresses. How I found myself surrounded by murderous-looking Arabs in a hashish den in the backstreets of a Moroccan Casbah. My experiences and serious participation in spiritualism. But still, these are other stories. There are enough in this book to suffice at this time.

By the time this is read, there is every possibility that I will be in Hollywood making my first film there, and if I know me, I'll find life where the life is. After all — that's life.

George Harrison Marks

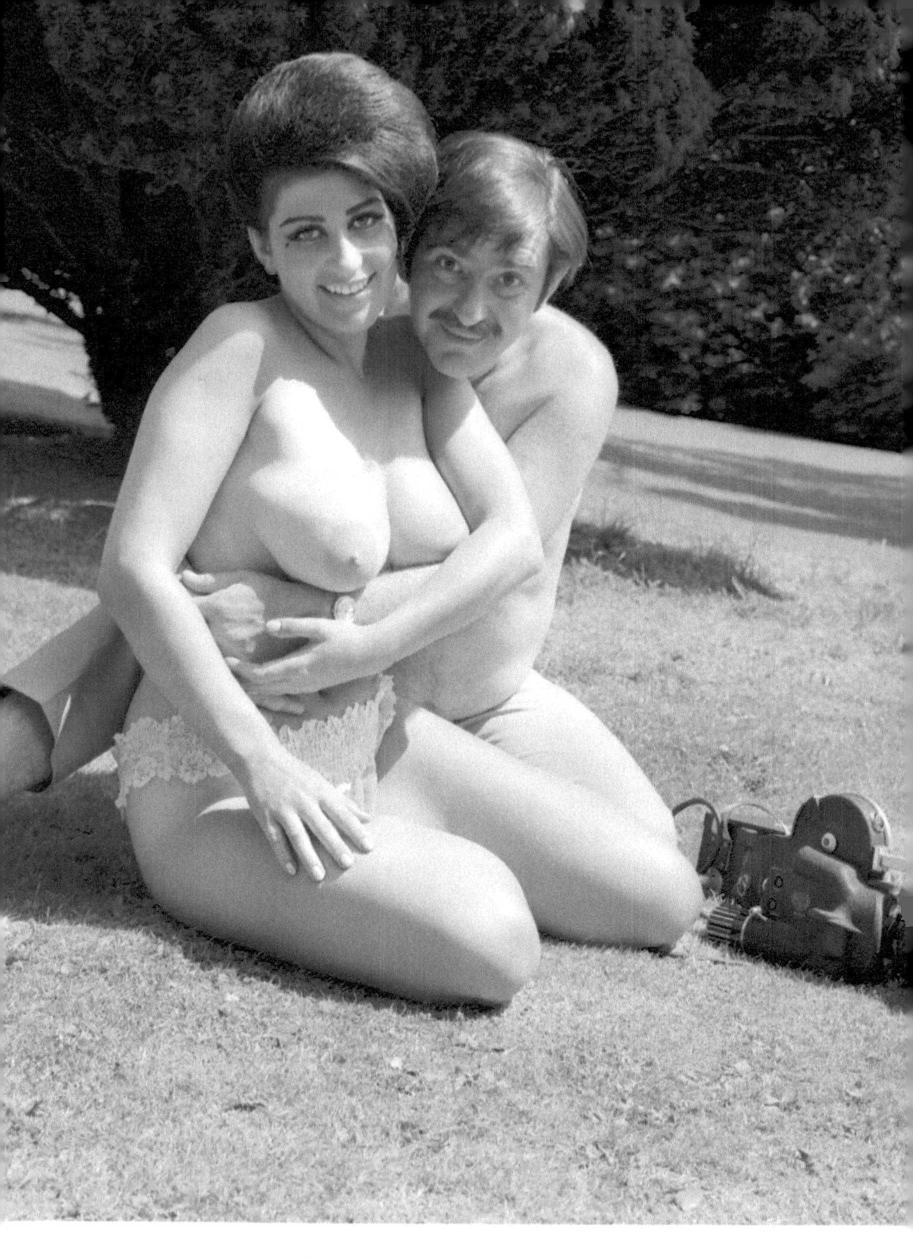

Monique Devereux and George Harrison Marks

CHAPTER 1

The World's Leading Nude Photographer

GEORGE Harrison Marks collects women like other men collect porcelain, paintings, cigarette coupons or trading stamps. He has observed in his working life more really beautiful women, naked as nature intended, than an average man could ever dream about in 1,000 years.

At 40, he is a connoisseur of female beauty; the pre-eminent nude photographer in the world.

But there is very much more to this man than just a bunch of pretty faces.

Women, though, are his dominant interest. He confesses: "I am lucky, they are my work as well as my hobby… and I love every moment I spend at both."

Through women, naked women, he has become rich, famous — even notorious. They have made him, and they have broken him. They have brought him happiness and love; and in almost equal proportions, disillusion and despair.

For the ordinary man, it is difficult enough to keep one woman happy. Harrison Marks keeps on splendid terms with hundreds a year. They work for him, they undress for him, their pictures are sent by the million round the world.

And, as a rule, they are not professional models. Mostly they are ordinary suburban girls; secretaries, receptionists, typists, housewives. They come from Kingston-upon-Thames and Kingston-upon-Hull; from Blackheath and Blackburn. In fact, they are the girls next door.

The Harrison Marks story reveals more about women than just their beautiful bodies and it also reveals more about the boys next door than the fact that they buy nude pictures, books and calendars by the million.

Harrison Marks is a man without cant or hypocrisy. He is as frank about his business as his pictures are about his models.

He is a lusty, hard-living man who says: “I adore beautiful women, I live for them, and I am completely dedicated to them.”

One question always is put to him. It comes in a variety of ways, often directly, mostly insidiously. “Be frank,” Mr. Marks, the questioners say, “do you sleep with your models? ‘

If he answers no, they don’t believe him; if he answers yes, they still don’t believe him.

In the first instance, they think he’s covering up and in the second instance, they think he’s boasting.

And often in the mind of the questioner, there is a predisposition to disbelief. A man who looks at a picture of a very beautiful naked girl frequently becomes emotionally involved with the image. He doesn’t like it if the answer is yes. In some curious way, it makes the girl in the picture unfaithful. It is a very private affair, this taking and, studying nude pictures.

A lot of people are prepared to put Harrison Marks down as a pansy. There is a fiction current among many film and photographic people, and it is often said: “Of course, he’s a raving queer.” Raving queer, or raving lecher, what is the truth?

“Well, the queer bit is a laugh, a big laugh,” says Harrison Marks. “The womanising can be overstated, too,” he explains. “In one year, five to six hundred girls go through my studios.

“I’m a bit of a goer… but that is ridiculous. “But, of course, I’ve had affairs with some of my models, deep emotional affairs.”

He points to the portraits in oils on the walls of his flat. “The artist who does those,” he says, “falls madly in love with every model he paints. Often he is suicidal about it. It breaks him up.

“I have fallen in love with some of my models, I work with them so closely, it’s only natural. Bosses in offices and industry fall in love with secretaries. And I’m much closer to my girls than that. The conditions we work under are probably ripe for an affair.

“But, remember, a lot of my models are respectably married women — and most of those very, very happily married. The fact that they are prepared to model shows that they are well-adjusted sexually.

“If it became a fact that I slept with all my models, or even tried to make them, nobody would work for me.

"I have more trouble with girls who try to make me. And later I will tell you about some of the incidents."

One other question always comes up: Is it art? Since the Renaissance right up to the time of the Impressionists and Abstracts, pictorial representation of the nude was regarded as the highest achievement in art. The ability to draw, paint or sculpt the human figure was the acid test of an artist's greatness. Pin-up artists like Vargas and Petts became famous, socially acceptable and respectable. Their work was often criticised as mechanical and photographic, but they were recognised as artists.

Yet for some reason photography of the nude figure has been considered salacious, unsavoury — even pornographic. Somehow, the public considers it a little too easy, like copying. It seems unfair that with a click and in 1/25th of a second the photographer can go a long way to getting the same results as the "true" artist. He hasn't obviously worked for it, struggled for the effect. Like the recent sign in a multiple store over batches of rather inferior oil paintings "painted by hand". That means they're real, genuine. They are done by hand, it implies, they must be good.

Harrison Marks says about his work: "I'm not going to dress it all up as arty one bit. Selling the sex image is my business, and I'm not ashamed of that. Men like to see pictures of beautiful girls in the raw state, and I give them what they like to look at, and I have made a lot of money doing it — and I'm not ashamed of that, either.

"I've been in the pin-up business for ten years or more and I suppose I must have seen more naked girls than the average man has had hot dinners, but the fascination of female beauty has never left me."

To him, it is undoubtedly art, commercial art, carried out to the exacting standards required in the field. As demanding as any advertising illustration.

"To me, a picture of a naked woman is as much a work of art as a photograph of a child, or a face or a cathedral.

"I am not," and he is very emphatic, "I am not in the pornography game."

"Any mug can take dirty pictures. I don't. And I don't need to, either for the money or the kicks. I take photographs of lovely girls, thousands of them, but I don't deal in smut."

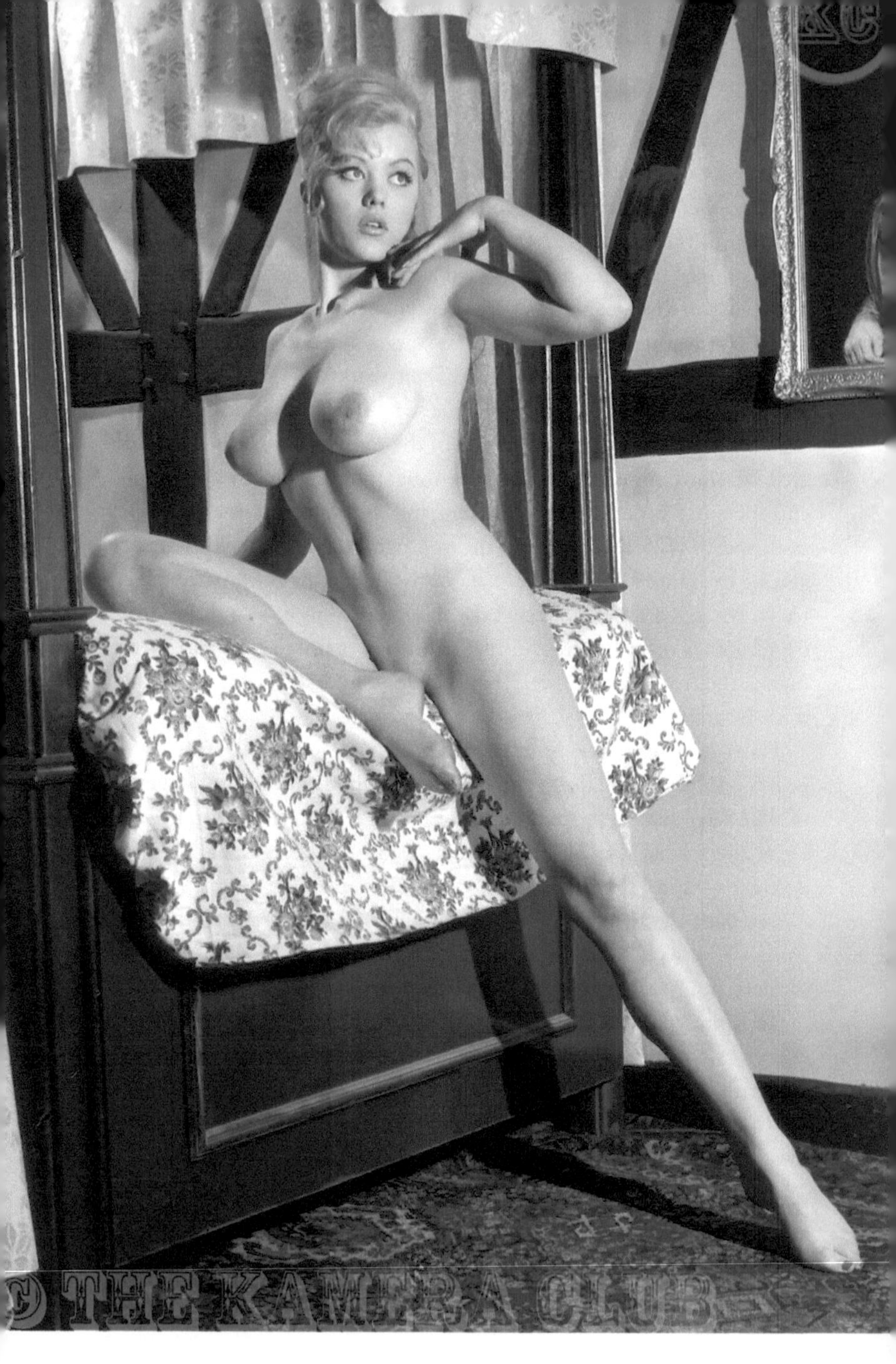
© THE KAMERA CLUB

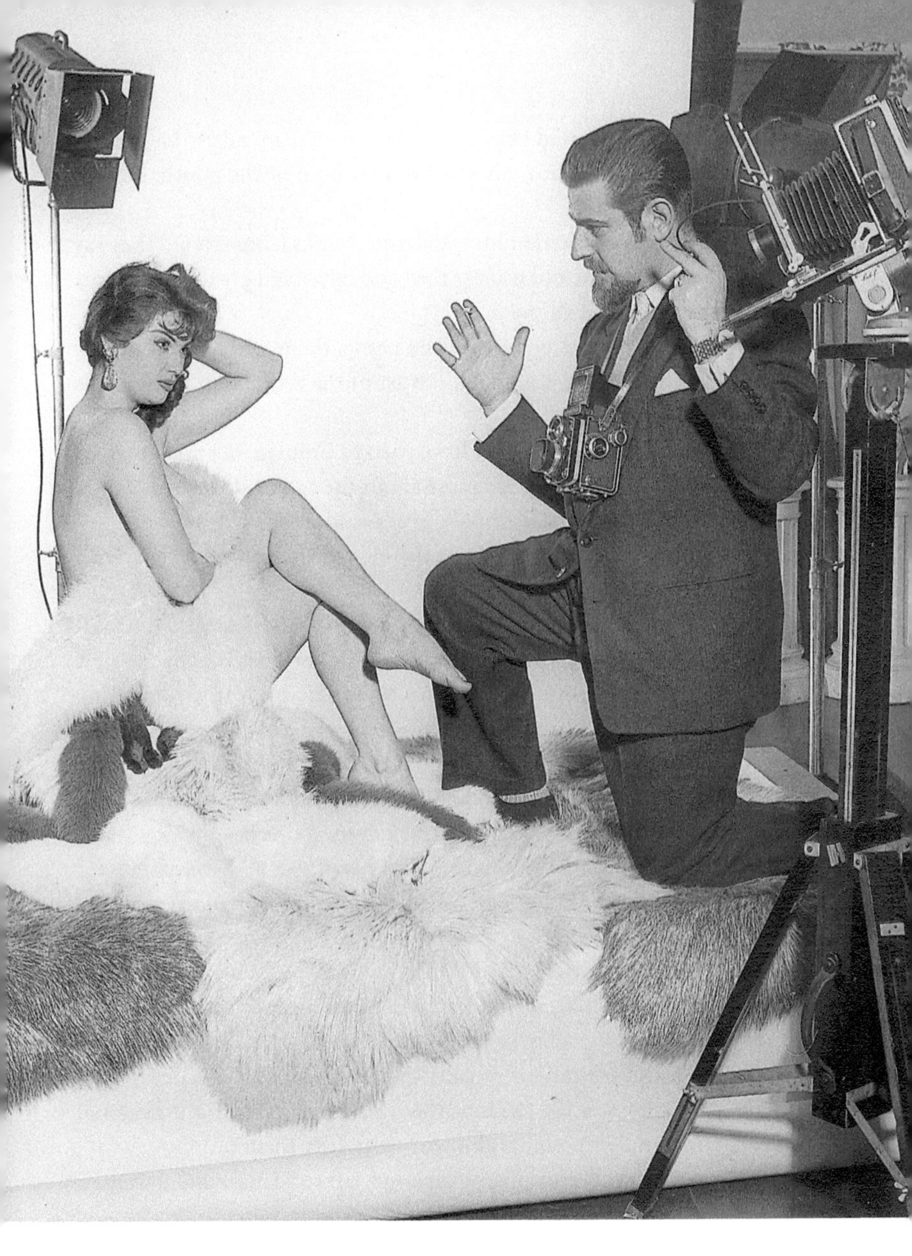

Above: George Harrison Marks lining up a shot with Eve Eden (Rosa Domaille)

Left: Margaret Nolan, a.k.a. Vicky Kennedy

Fine art has influenced Harrison Marks' work. Particularly he admires Sir William Russell Flint, and he resents some of the contemporary criticism of the artist.

"The arty boys condemn him," Harrison Marks comments. "They say that he is commercial and usually they add disparagingly that he 'paints nude women — and all that'.

"He certainly paints nudes, and he paints them with genius. In my view, he is the greatest watercolour artist of the century and as good as any there have ever been.

"His nudes are magnificent. I have tried to simulate my particular art on his work. He has taught me more about the composition of a picture than 1000 photographic textbooks ever could.

"At home, I have Russell Flint paintings in every room. They are a constant inspiration.

"Certainly sex appeal is the end product — the reason why I sell millions of nude pictures every year, but I do not subscribe to the view that sex is a dirty thing. As a matter of fact, I think it is something beautiful and that a picture of a female form in all its glory is a thing of beauty if it is properly done."

Equally certain, too, is the fact that many millions of people from Bishops and bankers to bakers and bricklayers appreciate his view of art and beauty. More than 50,000 copies of his magazine *Kamera* are sold every issue; about a million-and a-half copies of his colour calender are sold every year.

Latterly his film "The Naked World of Harrison Marks," has packed them in in London's West End for 14 continuous months.

Now it is showing all over the world, even in Japan.

Question number three is usually: "Where do all the girls come from?" Again somewhere at the back of the questioner's mind is a personal association and the thought "and why can't I get them?"

The answer reveals a lot about Harrison Marks and more about women as models and, to coin a phrase, romantic exhibitionists.

"I never chase after them," Harrison Marks explains.

"I have never, once, asked a girl to model — they always come to me. I have a turnover of about 600 girls passing through my studios every year, and I'll use perhaps 150 of them as models. So you see, I don't have to chase them."

A little wryly, he adds: "And I never chase after it, if you are thinking about sex."

Harrison Marks is 40, reasonably good-looking, black hair, a black moustache, tanned and fit. But really no Adonis and certainly not a film star image, say, in the mould of Errol Flynn or Tony Curtis.

His personality is, however quite dominant: lively, creative, good fun, bounding with energy. And women undoubtedly adore him.

The real secret of his success with women is that he does genuinely like and understand them, they sense it, and they respond.

"After all, this kind of work is a pretty intimate thing to start with. You have to make a friend of any girl you want to picture in the altogether. I can't say 'move over here, Miss. Just move your leg over a little, Miss'. I have to get friendly.

"A girl has to trust me when I'm taking her pictures or else the whole thing gets awkward, and the awkwardness shows through the camera, and that's no good to me. Any girl who works with me has to 'give', to relax and use her intelligence — because a dumb model is worse than useless.

"And so, if we spend an eight-hour session together, the model and I get through all the barriers of modesty and, quite often, beyond that towards an intimate relationship. Beyond that? Well, that's up to the girl, myself, and normal human behaviour.

"But one thing I do know. Some of the best pictures I have ever taken have been of girls I've been emotionally involved with. Maybe, it is only because I have been so attached to these girls that I think these pictures are great; there are pictures which I've taken of girls I have only ever shaken hands with of which I am proud. But, somehow, with those I have loved, well, there's a subtle look in their eyes, a light on their faces that shines through the picture to give it that indefinable something that makes a first-class nude photograph.

"It is the best way I know of making a girl feel on top of the world. And if you can make her feel a million dollars, put her on a pedestal, she will come over in the picture. That is the magic ingredient in a good pin-up — the pedestal bit, the unattainable.

"It's that which makes a man pin a picture to his wall and admire it; the thought that, really, the girl is too good for him and that he would never really be able to get to grips with someone like that. So he just dreams about it, and it makes him feel good to dream."

Harrison Marks' business is a fundamental trade and produces many fundamental truths. He deals in the commonest commodity which is often the most unobtainable, and he realises that his biggest selling point is the oldest problem in creation: the mystery of womanhood. He preserves it in his pictures — he pedals the dream, he sells the fancy, not the flesh.

"And that's the truth, isn't it?" he asks. "It's the other blokes' girl who fascinates you at a party — the one you don't know and can't have — no matter how lovely your own girlfriend is.

"It is that idea, I think, which sells a million and a half of my pin-up calendars every year and sells my magazines and pictures all over the world.

As he says, women have brought him success. "All the money for my needs"; with this goes a luxurious home, richly furnished in very good taste, complete even with its own sauna bath.

Expensive paintings hang on the walls; there are all the trappings of the good life. In the path of success there also came three wives, many mistresses and a multitude of friends nearly all famous household names.

Not bad for a man who left school at 13 and who, only 14 years ago, had ls. 4d. in his pocket.

Women are only part of the Harrison Marks story. In his time he has been a Bohemian, a film clapper-boy (and tea carrier), a street photographer and a music hall comic. He ran a dress mail order business. Once he even became a busker.

The lesson from Harrison Marks' life is that when the opportunities came, he grabbed them with enthusiasm and failure never really worried him.

His family has always had a theatrical background and his early life gave him training to be his own best impresario. "Once a ham, always a ham," he is fond of saying. He has spent much of his time trying to prove it.

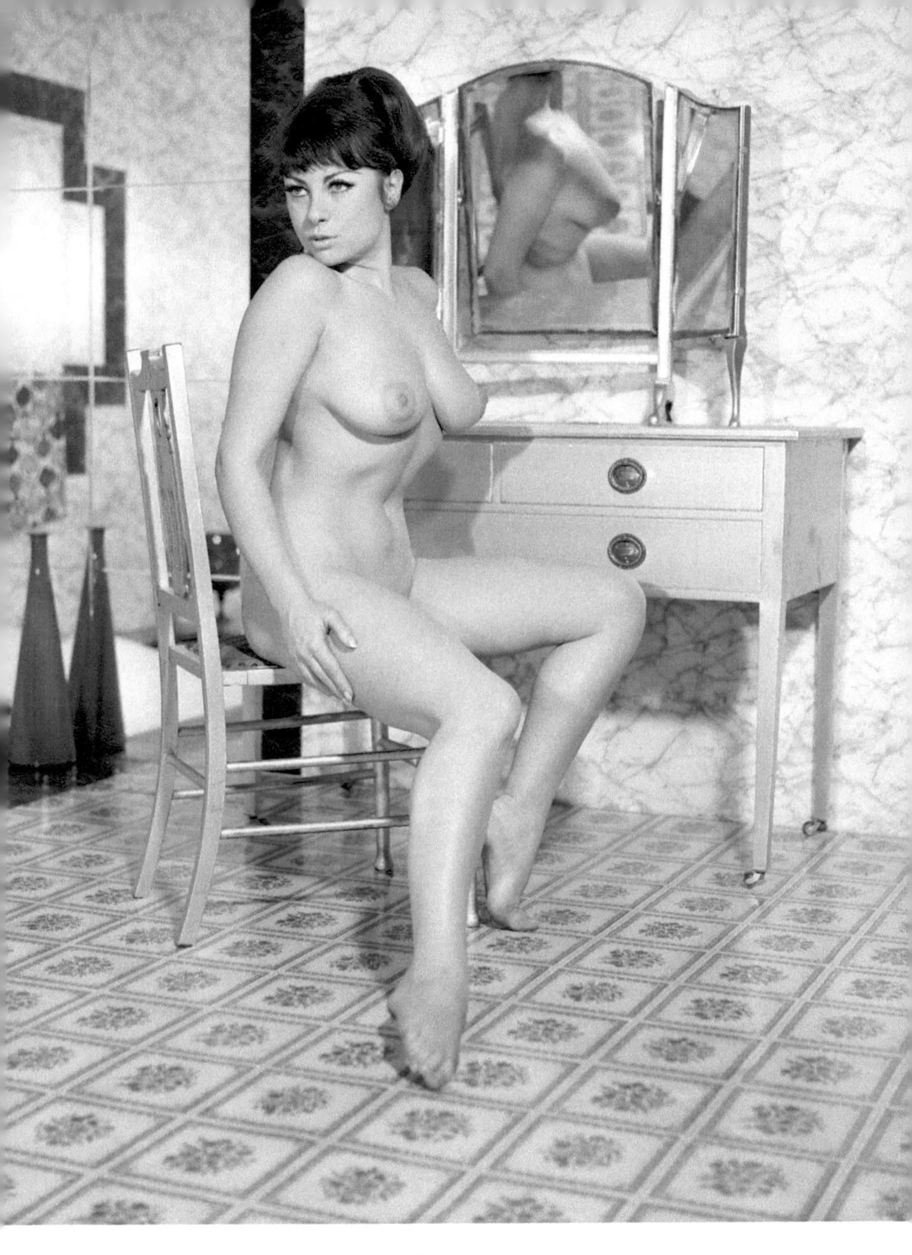

The ever professional June Palmer

CHAPTER 2

Birth, the Family

GEORGE Harrison Marks was born on Friday, August 6th, at 4.30 in the afternoon in Tottenham, London. A Leo, who turned out to be exactly what a Leo should be.

Nothing much else happened in the world on that particular day except that Warner Brothers launched the first ever talking picture.

The Marks family originated from the Spanish Jewry and have been established in London since 1711, Harrison Marks's father, a financier, with theatrical connections, had married late in life at 45. This was the first child and the young George, lying there with his ears sticking out like jug handles, was destined, or doomed, it depends on your point of view, to become the centre of attraction for his own and his father's large family of elder sisters, plus their husbands.

Jewish families cling tightly together, and there is always an acknowledged head of the Family. The leader. In this case, it was Aunt Esther, known in the family circle as the "sergeant major".

And Harrison Marks recalls his early life:

"Every Saturday without fail, the family were summoned to arrive at her home for lunch, tea and dinner, and as far as I can remember no one ever stayed away. Aunt Esther would stand at the head of the table, not so much serving the food, but commanding a military campaign, with the plates as artillery to be moved to the front line at the other end of the table. At her right hand would sit her husband, my Uncle Alf, carving an enormous chicken as if preparing ammunition, whilst at her left would sit poor Aunt Deborah whose duty it would be to pass the plates. She was always terribly flustered. I would sit in wonder watching the whole manoeuvre carried out with fantastic speed and precision, and although there were usually 10 or 12 sitting at the table, all seemed to receive their plates (which were always passed clockwise round the table) at the same time.

"Throughout the courses, although apparently fully occupied commanding at the table head, Aunt Esther seemed to me to have a form of second sight. She seemed to know in advance what I would be about to do. As if she were sounding the 'charge' she would bark, 'Georgie, elbows off the table' before they were ever there. Likewise, I was told the correct way to eat soup and handle the silverware.

"Eventually, I possessed impeccable table manners, but I longed to eat like the maids in the kitchen, elbows on table and a book propped up on a sauce bottle. By and large, it was a typical pre-war family circle.

"Nowadays Aunt Esther has mellowed — a little. The table has dwindled to herself, Uncle All and Aunt Deborah, all in their eighties. But Aunt Esther can still dole out instructions like the crack of a whip."

Father had a great leaning towards the Music Hall; he was passionately interested in all the artists. This had something to do with the fact that Great Aunt Florry had appeared with 'Little Titch' way back in the early part of the century. He belonged to a variety club, and on Sunday, although George was no more than three or four, he would be trundled along to the show — the highlight of the week for him.

Harrison Marks says about these visits: "I loved the atmosphere, the smell of cigars, the boisterous songs the professionals used to sing. To this day I can remember the adverts. On the stage Front Cloth there I would sit on the knees of many of the old-time 'greats' of the music halls.

"Back at home after these Sunday outings, I would make my father sing the songs I had heard over and over again until I knew them all by heart. I would watch the actions and imitate them.

"The following Saturday, after the family lunch, I would stand in the centre of the lounge and sing to my Aunts and Uncles. At the end of each song, I would insist on the whole company shouting more-more as the audience did at the variety club.

"Bless them; they never seemed to have enough of me standing there shouting my head off. In my own home, the case would be the same; any visitor would be saddled with Georgie Marks and his unintelligible songs. How those poor bastards must have suffered.

"Then came the day when one of the artists 'blacked up' for his performance."

It could have been G. H. Elliott, "the chocolate coloured coon", a great favourite of his from as far back as he can remember. And this sparked the first family crisis Harrison Marks can accurately remember.

"A few days later I came across an indelible pencil left lying around. I grabbed an egg cupful of water from the kitchen, and dived under the dining-room table which was covered with a heavy velvet cloth, dropping deep at the sides, to do my 'make up'. There I sat for a full hour while the family searched the house and garden for me.

"Aunts Esther and Deborah had turned up, and my presence was required. Wonderful, I thought, they can all see me. I rubbed myself all over with the pencil, face, neck, arms and legs.

All was set for my grand entrance. 'Here I is,' I bawled. I crawled out and stood up for the full effect. Ruth, the maid, who had been looking for me with the rest, was standing by the dining-room door. She stared stupidly at me for a moment and then fled… in terror.

"The rest is vague, but I know my Mother threw hysterics, Aunt Esther went for Ruth, just as Ruth had anticipated she would the moment she saw me, and Aunt Deborah went limp in a chair, and my Father went for the Doctor.

"To round off the afternoon, it seems that someone had sent for a Policeman earlier in the proceedings when they thought little Georgie was lost. He loomed up in the hallway during the pandemonium as I was rushed up to the bathroom.

"It took a week or so for Mother and the house to quieten down, to get the indelible ink off my skin, and for me to get back in the Family's good books."

The family life was soon disrupted. Suddenly, in the biting March winds in 1930, Father caught a chill. Pneumonia set in and within a week he died.

Harrison Marks says: "I feel now that this was the greatest loss of my life. Only now do I understand how much I missed the guiding hand, the love, and the friendship. As I grew older, I used to envy my friends who spoke of their fathers, and of the things they did together. I built a barricade within myself, against these incidents, and a picture grew in my mind of my father, a glowing, larger than life-size picture.

"Later I realized that he was obviously a very normal man, just the same as anyone else, but I can still feel a sense of pride, today, when I meet people who remember my old man, Moss Marks, with affection."

Even at five, no matter how great the shock, time heals and life soon took on its familiar routine. School started — disastrously. And the young George had his first experiences of sex. In the one case, in all sweet innocence; and in the other, not remotely knowing what was happening to him.

Could some psychologist trace his later undoubted fascination with the female body to experiences the infant Harrison Marks had with Ruth, the maid?

In all probability, yes.

But first, school.

From the very first day he hated it. In the first week, he ran away three times.

Poor favourite Uncle Rocky, a bachelor who had been a lifelong friend of Moss Marks and who took over part of young George's upbringing when his father died, spent a lot of his time, over the years, marching the unwilling boy back through the forbidding gates.

At school there were girls in the class. Here, for the first time, George fell madly in love.

The girl was Elsie. It all happened when they were made to stand together, in disgrace, behind the blackboard.

"My affection flared into passion," Harrison Marks recalls. "I planted a resounding kiss on her lips."

Miss Birdy, the teacher, exploded. She gave him a severe talking to and sent him to stand outside the classroom.

But the damage was done, Elsie was now his girl — forever. So, at the age of seven, dates the t "experience" in the Harrison Marks career. Ruth, on the other hand, was an entirely different flower in a forbidden garden.

"It was now that I saw the human body in its entirety for the first time," Harrison Marks says, adding: "Though, I must confess, it didn't inspire me as much as it had done in later years.

"I liked it well enough, however — if only because it gave me an excuse for staying up late."

Ruth was the general home help, who lived in. A pretty girl, well proportioned, she must have been 18 to 20 when she arrived. She settled down quickly as one of the family. Most evenings she had to herself, except for the times Mother Marks went out to friends or to the theatre. On those nights Ruth and young George were left together.

Harrison Marks' memory of the situation is this:

"We would have supper, and then I would have my bath before Ruth had her's. Afterwards, she would come into my bedroom and stand in front of the full-length mirror on the wardrobe, admiring her naked self.

"I was fascinated, as she primped and posed to her reflection, and after this regular performance she would drape her red dressing gown over her shoulders and sit on my bed.

"Then she would tell me — I really can't think why — ALL about her latest love affair, in the minutest detail.

"I hadn't the simplest idea what it was all about. Nevertheless, I liked it, the more she chattered, the longer I could stay awake.

"But there was one other thing about these sessions which I found quite fascinating.

"Ruth was sitting there, quite undressed except for the robe round her shoulders and as she talked she liked me to fondle and caress her breasts.

"I was intrigued that her nipples would contract and harden when I touched them. Apart from that, I had no interest — only to keep her talking.

"The other thing that appealed to me was that she always swore me to secrecy. I felt as if I was really in at a secret ritual. And the curious thing is that I've never mentioned it to anyone until now.

Ruth, sweet Ruth, soon lost her bloom. She found her man and there were whisperings between the adults, and odd sounding phrases like "in the family way" drifted through the house, followed by 'tut, tuts".

Ruth left rather quickly and so ended the somewhat premature sex education. But at least it meant that the son of the house got some early nights.

The young George was no precocious romantic, nor was he any sorts of scholar. But the business flare soon showed itself. And a business partnership started which has lasted, almost without break, ever since. Today it is stronger than ever and Harrison Marks' school-mate, Stuart

Samuels, is now his general manager at the Studio; Stuart is four months younger than Harrison Marks.

Now, he confesses, he looks older. Somehow he always seems to get just the worst of the deal; it seems that it was always so. Nowadays the studio "family" joke is about The Picture of Dorian Gray.

This reference comes from an incident much later in life when they were touring together on the music halls. In the same town, a touring company was doing Oscar Wilde's *Dorian Gray*, and they were sharing the same digs. The talk was about the play, and how successful it was and Stuart looked a little puzzled.

Quietly he asked Harrison Marks: "What kind of an act is this Dorian Gray, anyway?"

"You silly sod," George replied. "It is a straight play." And they sat up all night while he explained the plot. The story fascinated Stuart and became engrained in his mind.

Nowadays George lives, as he readily admits, quite a hell-raising life. The candle burns at both ends and in the middle, and when one candle is finished, another is quickly lighted. All the vices are there: wine, women and song in plenitude.

Still, he looks fit, bronzed, active, alive and very, very healthy. Stuart, on the other hand, lives a quiet, domesticated and sober life… and looks older, paler and a little sadder each day.

After the heaviest nights, George comes bouncing into the studio full of beans and raring to go. After the quietest night at home, Stuart will arrive tired, a little rough at the edges and ten degrees under.

When he is not feeling so well Stuart says: "Get the picture out." And he adds ruefully: "It's so bloody unfair, George, you wicked devil; everything you do shows on ME!

"Do me a favour — have an early night, will you? I'm not feeling so good, and I can't stand the strain."

Still, the partnership has lasted since schooldays.

The first meeting came about on the way home from school. They stopped to study the remains of a piece of haddock in the gutter and agreed precisely that it was a lump of fish. There and then a friendship was cemented, which has lasted to this day. Harrison Marks, being the senior, made the decisions. Stuart has never failed to follow happily wherever the Harrison Marks schemes have led, be they fishy, fleshy or plain red-herrings.

With a length of string, a box, and Stuart as essential equipment, the business ventures began. They ended in disaster.

Number one came to mind after three sacks of fresh; steaming horse manure had been delivered to the Harrison Marks home. They arrived on a hand-cart, in an aura of what has been termed "a healthy stench" and Mrs. Marks handed over three large silver coins. The mercenary young Marks realized they were worth considerably more than the small brown pieces he occasionally received as an incentive to being a good boy, and knew beyond doubt, as he says, that they would buy a quantity of commodities such as gob-stoppers, sherbet, liquorice laces, or the funny wooden pellets you placed into a glass of water and watched blossom out before your very eyes, into beautiful flowers.

How simple it all was. The streets were strewn with silver. The milkman's, the coalman's, the baker's horses were all potential money-earners.

Harrison Marks well remembers the scheme: "I rushed round to play with Stuart, and, without going into exact detail, persuaded him to purloin the highly polished brass fireside shovel from the dining-room. Next, a call was made to Goldberg's, the Grocers. From this kindly gentleman we acquired a small cardboard box and a piece of string. Making holes in the box flap, I threaded the cord through, thus making a form of wheel-less carriage which could be pulled along the road. All tools assembled, away we went: I pulled the conveyance, Stuart marched at my side, shouldering the shovel.

"Through the streets, we tramped till we struck gold. And here, business relations became a little edgy. My partner was reluctant to shovel. I pointed out that it was his mother's shovel, and that, as such, he should do the shovelling.

"Stuart shovelled!

"With each fresh find, Stuart became even more disagreeable and in fact demanded that he should take a turn at pulling. Mutiny! It was my idea and consequently I should be driver. But the reasoning failed to convince. Suddenly Stuart swung out with the shovel — I know he didn't intend to hit me but merely to assert his position. At that moment, however, it meant but one thing – it was War!

"I had no weapon, but at my feet ammunition lay a-plenty. Picking up the box, I cradled it in my arm and, with my free hand, scooped out a handful and threw it! The effect was devastating Stuart burst into tears. Excited by my speedy victory, I gave him a second volley. He turned tail and fled down the road bellowing. I pursued, scattering our business in my wake.

"The second commercial venture arose through the cigarette-card collecting. The craze had swept the school, and the kids became fanatical in their search for new issues. Stuart and I were no exception. I, however, realised that I would have more chance of 'swaps' and that my social standing in the playground would go up if I had a more extensive range.

"I haunted my uncles for their empty packets and commanded Stuart to do the same. But this never seemed to give us the necessary bulk. And then one day I dreamed up an idea — if I could offer some service to my classmates, something that would be hard to refuse, they would pay in 'fag-cards' and we would be in business.

But what to offer? Rummaging through relics of forgotten summers, suddenly the manure box came to light. To give Stuart credit, according to Harrison Marks, he showed no sign of animosity at the sight of it. Clearly, here was the solution to the problem.

"In class the following day," Harrison Marks says, "I announced that following school I would give rides in my new chariot. Embarkation point: the back of my house.

"That afternoon, feeling like the Pied Piper, followed by Stuart, I arrived home with about 14 'punters'. With pride I pulled the conveyance out on to the pavement and announced to the gathering that for a fee of three cigarette-cards I would give each and everyone a ride. No eager anticipation showed on the faces of the prospective passengers, except for little Siddy Solomans, standing neatly in his sailor suit, who stepped forward. Gingerly, he lowered himself into the box, his behind wedged in, legs and arms dangling over the edge.

"Away we went, I pulling with all my might, Stuart pushing from behind. Without a doubt, it was a great success. Siddy squealed with delight as I dragged him to the end of the street and back. Immediately others thrust their cards forward to be next.

"I had noticed as Siddy came out of the box that the bottom having stood on the damp floor of the shed, had rotted slightly, and the friction of the cardboard against paving stones, had worn a hole through. Siddy's pants were now slightly the worse for wear.

"These were but trivialities and business was brisk and off we went again.' One passenger followed another, each having two, three, even four rides. Now there was hardly any bottom left in the box, but who cared? The fun was fast and furious.

"At the end of possibly two hours, the conveyance went U.S. The speed of pulling had also shown signs of weakening, so we put up the shutters and called it a day, with the promise that we would get a new 'chariot' for the morrow. And so a group of weary, happy children wended their way home, with the arses of their trousers hanging in tatters.

"Later that evening, my Mother was summoned to the front door where stood Mrs. Solomans, waving the remains of Siddy's pants. Two further visits from irate parents followed, and another the next day. The small packet of cards I had earned that, afternoon, eventually cost the house of Marks one sailor suit and four pairs of trousers.

Apart from Stuart, my circle of regular playmates were children living in the same avenue as ourselves.

"Leslie was a little boy with golden hair and the face of an angel, but with one curious idiosyncrasy, which made him the horror of the neighbourhood — he had a fanatical mania for flowers. No garden was safe from the plucking fingers of Leslie. On his way home from school each afternoon, he would make lightning visits to front gardens along the way, picking choice blooms as he went. No matter how many hidings he received, he would not, or could not, stop. Flower beds for streets around were stripped bare by his efforts. At the end of each raid when he was, more or less, in the safety of his own garden, he could always be heard singing a popular song of the day in which a line of the lyrics went 'Come and pick flowers with me'. As far as I know, nobody ever took up the offer, but it did serve as a warning for people to make sure their garden gates were securely fastened.

"Then there was Cyril Datlow, brother of Elsie, the girl I fell madly in love with that day at school when we were both made to stand in disgrace behind the blackboard. He was a little younger than I, with nothing out of the way for me to remember him for, except that he was his mother's pride and joy, and this led to 'The Battle of Wellington Avenue'. This is how it happened:

"Two other lads with whom I spent a great deal of my early years were the Winters brothers, Mike and Bernie, the TV comedians. Their family, a large and lively group, came to live in Wellington Avenue when I was about seven. Mike and I were the same age and became firm friends, spending a great deal of time in each other's homes. Bernie, because he was slightly younger than we were, became something of a hindrance, and we would contrive numerous ways to lose him if he tagged along with us. This would be impossible today since he now dwarfs us by about a foot. Actually, he comes from a line of enormous men. The Winters boys' two uncles were giants, one being the Great Jack Bloomfield. I remember sitting in silent wonder gazing up at those two men and wishing I could boast such uncles as Mike did, a sure guarantee of immunity from School Bullies.

"The fighting spirit, however, seemed to run through the family, and it caused the 'Battle'.

"One morning Cyril. Datlow and Bernie Winters were playing together when a quarrel started. Cyril, although the older, fared the worse. Defeated and tearful, he ran home. Now, as I have said, Cyril, in his mother's eyes, was the original cherub, and on seeing the conquered warrior, feathers flew. She stomped down the road to find Bernie and give him a severe telling off plus a smack on the arm.

"Mrs. Winters, hearing that her son had been given a 'good hiding', flew from her house, down the road to the Datlow residence. But Mrs. Datlow was out shopping. By this time, the children who were playing nearby, hearing the 'shindig going on up and down the Avenue, had left their games and were now waiting for the fun to start.

"After some time, the unfortunate Mrs. Datlow appeared, laden with numerous carrier-bags. Bernie, who had been swinging on his garden gate all afternoon, jumped down and ran into the house.

"No doubt, Mrs. Winter had by this time cooled down, and without this reminder there would have been possibly a few harsh words the following day and peace would have reigned, but with the reappearance of Sonny Boy so soon after the event, her fury flared again, and she charged out of the front door ready for all comers.

"The unsuspecting Mrs. Datlow glanced up and saw the angry Mme. Winters bearing down on her. There was a loud and very heated exchange of words, and suddenly self-control snapped. Mrs. Winters made a grab at the nearest carrier-bag and scattered the contents all over the road. The other packages followed suit. Mrs. Datlow, the loser from the word go, decided that a speedy retreat was the order of the day, and with the victor in close pursuit, ran home as fast as her legs could carry her.

"Never in all our lives had we kids ever seen anything like it. All around lay the wreckage strewn over the road and pavement: apples, oranges, fish, plums, meat, stockings, pickled cucumbers, groceries of every description were amongst the debris. The majority of us were too well mannered (or scared) to pick them up, but others had a beano, and soon no evidence remained to tell that the Battle had taken place. Little Siddy Soloman sat on the edge of the kerb stuffing himself on a large bag of plums. But retribution came to him in the right and proper way. In the 'little room of his home, he remained 'glued' to the mahogany seat during the following two days."

Perhaps the firmest indication of Harrison Marks' future talent came from his friendship with a boy bearing the distinguished name of Nobby Clark. Nobby was a trusting lad, and young George tried his first attempt at cinematographic direction with him.

It came after a scripture lesson at school. Harrison Marks recalls "I listened to the lesson in which we were told Christ walked upon the water. The moral of the story was Faith, and for some reason, I thought that anyone with sufficient trust could work wonders as well. I selected Nobby as my candidate and took him home with me after school. Taking him up to my bedroom, I showed him that, from the window, the roof of the greenhouse was but a step away. Leaving him sitting on the sill, I ran down to the garden and stood in the centre of the lawn. In the most saintly voice, I could command I told Nobby to walk. He stepped off onto the glass roof and stood, slightly bent at the knees, with an expression of extreme fear on his face. 'Walk, Nobby,' I called up, but poor Nobby lacked sufficient faith. As he took the next step, there was a crack, a shattering of glass, and my disciple crashed through, disappearing 12 feet into the depths below."

Only one phrase is really apt in comment: "Cut!" And it was one Harrison Marks was to use often in his later career — only in the film-making sense.

CHAPTER 3

Marriage at Seventeen

IT was 1939, and the lights were going out all over Europe, including Tottenham. But for one young fellow of 13, the light from the torch of freedom burned with a dazzling intensity. Schools closed and scholars were evacuated and dispersed. So Master George Harrison Marks arranged for his own dispersal, right out of the orbit of the education authorities… forever.

For a time no one really knew where the children were, and that suited the unwilling scholar fine. He became a fugitive from formal education and took a job helping the projectionist at the Regal Cinema, Wembley.

There were moments of tension and doubt. About this time the school leaving age was raised to 15, and young George spent an anxious year dodging down back alleys to avoid anybody who looked remotely like a Schools Attendance Officer.

He survived. Then came his first big break. Answering an advertisement in the situations vacant columns of the *Evening Standard*, he got an appointment — as a tea-boy at Ealing Studios.

This was the first really constructive move in the Harrison Marks career. For the first time he wanted to learn, desperately he wanted to learn and the memories of those early days in Ealing are indelibly stamped on his memory.

It set the seal on his ambition. He knew then just what he wanted to do. Today it is just the same, 26 years later the first ambition is still valid most of all, he wants to make films. Here is how he describes the first awakening:

"I loved that job from the first day, even though it amounted to little more than fetching tea for the film-makers. It got into my system then, and it produced a kind of fever which has gripped me ever since.

"Just to stand and watch those old pictures being made — films with Will Hay and Tommy Trinder and all the Ealing comedy stars — filled me with great excitement. I wanted to know everything about everything and I asked questions, got in the way and probably made a horrible nuisance of myself, but I had a great itch to do all these things myself — that's just me. And I did learn a lot. Gradually, I was allowed to move into the production side in a small way, yet it wasn't until the war overtook everything that I really had the chance to move into the actual photography bit.

"It started with the National Film Service where, incidentally, I met the man who made the first-ever moving picture in this country, Cecil Hepworth. He was pretty old then, but just seeing him was a sort of thrill which I can't explain, except that it was the kick of rubbing shoulders with one of the 'greats' of the business.

"It was with Universal News, however, that I really began to learn all about the business of movie photography and just about everything else. And I learned at the hands of a master of the art, Percy Mumford, a cameraman who knew everything there was to know about it and who had been in the game for decades.

"To have had that opportunity makes me the luckiest guy I know. Percy took a liking to me and decided to teach me all the tricks and techniques of his trade and no man anywhere knew them better."

It was a curious sight; the old man, doyen of the business, the brash, enthusiastic schoolboy being almost a shadow to him and certainly acting as his legs and arms.

The old man really did take a liking to young George, and the boy learned in the finest of all traditions, that of master and apprentice.

Mumford told him all the secrets, but one he kept back, and this one he didn't tell to a soul. George stumbled on it almost accidentally.

Harrison Marks: "Really, I shouldn't have been doing half of the things I did, but the war was on, and staff was short.

"I was only a studio assistant, yet he took the time and trouble to explain all the finer points to me. We were mainly concerned in filming interviews every week — the sort of shot-in-the-arm war effort bits such as speeches by Churchill, Eden and all sorts of war leaders, which went out into the cinemas with the newsreels. So I was given the chance to learn about studio lighting, sound, the whole camera operating technique, plus the technical mysteries of making film.

"Even at that stage, I couldn't understand why Percy was so keen to tell me all he knew. He simply said he was going to do it, adding: 'Keep it quiet, boy. I'll teach you all I know, but it's best you don't make a big thing of it. Keep it secret. Just learn.'

"Well, I always loved a secret, as you now know through Ruth. I kept my mouth tightly shut."

So it went on with young George setting up the camera for focussing and doing all the tasks which normally assistant cameramen would do… if it happened now there would be an immediate down-tools.

Mumford's secret dawned on Harrison Marks in a flash one day. He pointed something out to the old man who took a long time to pick it up. Impatiently young George thought, "the blind old bat".

The thought stuck, and he looked closely and carefully at Mumford. He saw the clear eyes staring ahead quite vacantly, for once, Mumford was off guard.

"My God," Harrison Marks thought to himself, "he is going blind."

It was true. Mumford's eyesight was failing — he was losing the only physical asset he really needed.

Instantly, Harrison Marks realised to himself, "I am his eyes."

Eyes can reveal far more than the tongue will ever tell. But in this case there was a conspiracy of silence between voice and vision, the secret never leaked.

There were great excitements at Universal as Harrison Mark recounts:

"We were working late one evening up on the third-floor studio at Universal in Wardour Street, shooting a great long row of medals laid out on red velvet. Maybe that sounds a push-over, but it involved some close camera work tracking all the way down the strip. It would not have been so bad had not there been a violent air raid going on at the time. And they were really dropping that night. The sounds of explosions were like a roll of drums, and the building shook every half a minute as the bombs went off. So, it took us hours to do, since every time Percy tried tracking, a bomb would go off, and the camera shook, and the whole thing had to be started again.

"In the end, he gave up. 'I can't do the job in the middle of this bloody lot,' he said. 'I'm knocking off.' The studio director was tearing his hair to get it done, but Percy was obviously right and he finally won his point, and we left.

"I had just reached Piccadilly Circus underground when there was a hell of a bang from not far away, followed by a whole series of others. And the next morning, when I turned up for work I found nothing but a heap of bricks lying where the Universal building had been — and where I had been, five minutes before the bomb hit the place."

Then there was the day when he "nearly put paid" to President Benes, the then President of Czechoslovakia.

"For the first time I was acting as clapper-boy, and when the time came for me to do my clapperboard bit, the President was talking to one of his advisors, although he was already sitting behind the studio desk in readiness for his interview.

"Unfortunately, he wasn't ready for me. I clapped the board down with enthusiastic force and the sudden sharp bang right next to his ear made the old man leap off his chair. They had to stop the whole production for half an hour while they gave him a glass of water and tablets and God knows what else to calm his nerves 1."

After the Universal building had been blown to pieces, Universal took up temporary residence in the Gaumont-British shop down the street. This was all right as an emergency operation but because they did not have a studio there was nothing for Harrison Marks to do and within three weeks he had been drafted to another job under the Control of Labour regulations.

"There was no arguing about it, either," he says. "And I found myself dumped in a film lab. doing the worst, the most boring and tedious job I have ever had to do in my life.

"For three months, I worked in a room completely on my own, with a camera which imposed sub-titles on to films. To start with, the titles were all in foreign languages, but the sheer tedium of the job was enough to send anyone crackers inside a week. There I was with this camera and a stack of blank cards with the sub-titles written at the bottom. The instruction on the back of each card gave the sequence and the number of frames in which the subtitle was to be imposed.

"Consequently, the job consisted of putting a card into a slot, pressing a shutter lead the right number of times, taking the card out, putting in the next and repeating the process *ad infinitum*. I was bored with it inside an hour, actively fed up with it at the end of a day, hating it at the end of a week and rebelling against it inside a fortnight. I mean, it was something out of Chaplin's *Modern Times* where workers spent their lives doing the same tiny operation over and over and over again.

"Anyhow, I kicked up hell about this job with the boss of the laboratory and at first, he just told me to shut up and get on with it since he couldn't do anything about it, it was war-time and all labour was controlled. But I made such a bloody nuisance of myself that they racked their brains to find a way to get rid of me. And at last, the lab. manager found a loophole through which I could get out. If they could show that I was totally unsuited to the job, he said, he might be able to get me released.

"In short, we agreed I'd drop a few monumental clangers

"I was more than ready to do this — anything to get out — but I had a stroke of luck just then. I got a bad case of ulcers and anyone who regards that as luck is pretty damned desperate, believe me 1 I'm quite sure that it was doing this job all alone and fretting about it that gave me the ulcers in the first place, so it was only right that through them, I was given a discharge from the place.

Chinese torture, Harrison Marks called that job. "There were stacks of cards standing as high as a man. Every time I got down to the last dozen, I'd think: That's it, thank God.

"Then the door would burst open and, bang — piles and piles and piles more."

There is, however, a delightful ironic twist to the story. The film laboratories were just off Tottenham Court Road.

Nowadays, Harrison Marks does some £50,000 worth of business with them every year.

Oxford Street is a great wide thoroughfare and the wind can blow terribly cold down either side of it. Harrison Marks claims expert knowledge of it.

The ulcers had cleared up, the memory of the Chinese drip torture had dimmed and, even though he had not got a job, life looked brighter for young George. As so often happened, opportunity smacked him in the eye.

"I happened to be walking with a girl down Oxford Street one Sunday afternoon," he explains, "when a street photographer snapped our picture and came up to us, giving us the old spiel — 'three for a dollar, a lovely picture of you and the girlfriend' and all that stuff. Of course, at the end of the war, it was difficult to get film, and having your picture taken was a novelty. So I stopped and dug out five bob and while I was giving the bloke my name and address, I was telling him I was in the film business but was out of a job."

Jimmy MacNeil, the photographer, looked him up and down. "Friend," he said," here's a Leica, get over the other side of the road and work the pitch outside Mooney's pub — there's enough graft in Oxford Street for both of us."

He was in business again. And rare business it proved to be for three or four months. A whole day's work could be done in the morning, 5s. for a click.

The pitch was good, but unfortunate. Even in an English summer the feet can get terribly cold. Lunchtime was spent in Mooney's "warming up".

What was the point of working in the afternoon?

Chances were anyway that after 3.0 p.m. the pictures wouldn't be very much in focus.

Winter killed the job. Enthusiasm dropped with the temperature. Where was the fun taking pictures with freezing fingers? When an east wind is whistling round their ears, people are reluctant to stop and give a name and address.

Also there are inherent dangers in dodging backwards trying to chat them up and give them the spiel.

"Just a minute guy. Just a minute. Come on, lovely picture of you and the girlfriend (wife). Three for five bob — make a beautiful Christmas card — only five bob for three .. . all right, piss off, then."

Of course, it could be somebody else's wife or girlfriend. The fact is that somehow winter induces a meanness in people.

You can see the distrust in their faces. Five bob on a hot, sunny day is one thing, who cares? But when it's freezing you can almost hear them think, "there's nothing in that camera; he's just trying to con me. I'll give him the five bob and that's the last I'll hear of that. He must think I'm a mug."

A provident street vendor would adopt a squirrel-like attitude and store up for the bitter season. Not Harrison Marks, its hard to accumulate when you are working outside a Mooney pub and you have a predisposition to thirst.

All that Harrison Marks desperately wanted was to be the spiel who came in from the cold.

Meanwhile, he had chummed up again with his bosom pal of schooldays, Stuart Samuels.

They went to a lot of parties together at the time — "Nearly always we'd find ourselves putting on a sort of spontaneous double-act — lots of patter, a bit on my banjo and a song, which always went down well amongst our friends," Harrison Marks says.

From the age of three, there had been a strong streak of the ham in G.H.M. and, almost compulsively, wherever George went, Sam was bound to follow.

"One night a bloke came over to us when we had done our bit and shoved his card at me — he was a theatrical agent.

"You in the business?" he said. "You working?" "Of course not," I said. "We're just amusing ourselves."

"Look, boy," the little chap replied, "I can get you work. If you're interested, give me a call."

"Well, I thought he must be damned hard up for a bit of commission and I didn't really take it seriously and thought no more about it."

It is easy now to see why winter so utterly defeated Harrison Marks. In his present home in St. Johns Wood, he lives in a perpetual hot-house; it is usually around 78 degrees. If that becomes too chilly — well, there's the sauna bath.

Clearly, he abominates cold. So one wet, dreary afternoon when George had retreated from the rigours of a morning's work in Oxford Street and he and Samuels were drinking Scotch in Mooney's, searching the numbed recesses of his mind, he turned to Stuart and said: "What about that bloody little theatrical agent? Let's go and see him. What can we lose? It'll be warmer in his office than the street."

One hour later, both began to wonder what on earth they had done.

The agent moved fast. They were booked to appear in a variety bill at the Granville Theatre, Walham Green. Topping the bill: Ernie Lotinga.

Harrison and Stuart had been launched, but there was a problem. They hadn't got an act.

Out they went and told Jimmy MacNeil that George was quitting to go on the boards.

It must have been something of a shock for him, too. He retired to Worthing, where he still works the sea front.

Down there, it's much safer — far less chance of meeting a real "nutter".

Before we go into the story of the Harrison and Stuart partnership in variety, let us recap a little. There were two things which happened between. George Harrison Marks leaving school and starting the theatrical career which profoundly influenced his life. The first was his introduction to women from a more interesting viewpoint, shall we say, than previously; the second was the launching of his matrimonial career.

So, first things first: the time when Mary raped him.

"How old was I at the Regal, in Wembley?" Harrison Marks asks. "Well, I suppose I was all of thirteen and eleven-twelfths or fourteen and one month; if anyone had asked me I would definitely have said fifteen-and-a-half. They weren't going to catch me on the school-age lark, I can assure you. Anyway, it was at that time of growing up when every day is of vital importance and every hour, you imagine, adds to your stature.

"I looked older and I acted older than I was. It's a funny thing, but I wasn't sexually precocious. In fact, my interest principally lay in the cinema and theatre. Because of my present work, a lot of people assume that I was born a raving, sex-mad lunatic. I wonder why they don't think the same about Rubens?

"At the Regal, in Wembley, there was, obviously, an usherette. All the older girls were away doing war-work and Mary was about 17. At work we saw a lot of each other and she took a great fancy to me. She was always hanging around. I didn't mind; she was someone to talk to and I always like an audience.

"One night, after the last show, she said: 'Why don't you walk me home?' All right,' I agreed. I didn't really give it a thought.

"In those days, all the railings round public places had been taken away to be melted down for war material. So the park was wide open and we walked across it.

"Halfway across, she stopped and asked: 'Aren't you going to kiss me?'

" 'OK,' I said. 'If you want me to, sure.' I made it sound like a chore. In fact, I did rate it just about at that level. Let's put it this way, I wasn't frantically enthusiastic, you know. I could take it or leave it.

"The next few minutes, however, fundamentally changed my mind. I kissed her and, whoomp, in a flash she had dragged me into the bushes. I was terrified. In the first place, I didn't know what to do. In the second place, I was sure that the 'parkie' or a special constable would catch us. I had got a terrible feeling at the back of my mind that you could be locked up for messing about with girls… in the dark… and in the park.

"I often wonder how much you can really remember of your first experience. In my view, young girls know a hell of a sight more about it than ever young boys do. Biologically, they must do. But in my experience they, not the boys, are generally the hunters . And they are the teachers, too. I have a strong suspicion that all the letters in women's magazines about 'first night difficulties' and things not quite clicking between young couples, are all aimed at young men. And I'll bet more young men than girls write to 'Auntie X' enclosing a S.A.E. for 'confidential advice'.

"Well, this was my very first experience. The moment when I began to realise what Ruth was all about.

"The girl must have had four pairs of arms. She put my hands everywhere and her hands were simultaneously all over the place. It was, of course, the era of buttons. Come to think of it, a lot of fun must have gone out of it with zips.

"What I remember most vividly was my ears: they were burning, red hot; they felt as if they would burst.

"Astonishingly I didn't fail. She sighed and for the first time I knew a woman's tenderness.

"She would have lingered, but all I wanted was to get home. I must get home. It was urgent. It was compellingly urgent. There was no time for lingering, no time for small talk. Home it had to be — or die.

"The romantic parting came like this: 'See you,' I blurted out and I galloped off. On the way back, the park had stretched at least three times as wide. "Her perfume clung. It encased me like a personal cloud. My suit reeked of the stuff and my lips tasted of it. As I ran, I went hot and cold in waves. My heart pounded, racing like a wild thing — then appeared to stop altogether. Fear, shame, fear again, embarrassment, humiliation — every emotion except happiness swept over me. I imagined her sitting on her bed and rolling with laughter and telling everybody at work all about it.

"At home, I ran a full, steaming hot bath; to hell with a four-inch limit — which was then law to save fuel — I poured in half a bottle of Izal, grabbed a tablet of Lifebuoy soap and scrubbed for an hour. I emerged boiled and smelling like Emergency Ward 10.

"The perfume was still on my suit, so I hung it in front of an open window. I collapsed into bed and fell into a dead sleep, and it wasn't until the morning that I thought about it again.

"There was a marked change in attitude. 'Well,' I thought, 'that wasn't bad. In fact, it was exciting.' The thinking about it was even better than the experience. I took, for the first time, a new vital interest in myself in the mirror. The whole thing was, I concluded, really very interesting. My thoughts fixed on Mary. There were mysterious things about her. Suddenly I remembered quite a lot about Ruth and connected it all with Mary.

"Curiosity, once aroused, is a dynamic force to a questioning mind, and my mind has always questioned. There followed an intense study of the Oxford dictionary. All that did was to confuse the issue and stimulate an even greater curiosity.

"Let me admit it; I had great qualms about turning up at the Regal. Flutterings in the tummy and hot flushes round the neck. But, wonders, Mary smiled; a big warm smile and batted her eyes at me. She was friendly. I looked at her and thought 'You're my Oxford dictionary and my Encyclopaedia Britannica'. The quest for knowledge was on.

"But, hang on a minute, it wasn't quite as smooth as all that. I almost forgot to tell you of the terror I went through for a couple of weeks. I am sure that every young boy suffers the same apprehensions after his first affair. At this time they were rather over-emphasised.

"Remember, the war was on, and the tube stations were plastered with Ministry of Health advertisements about the dangers of V.D. The advertisements were extremely bold and caused some people great embarrassment — though most were aware of the necessity for them.

"For instance, a mother brought her young daughter onto the platform of a tube station one day when I was there and the youngster said: 'What does it mean, Mummy — Beware V.D.?' And the mother replied, to her credit: 'It means beware of Vitamin Deficiency and that if you don't drink up your orange juice you'll be very ill… you might even die.'

"Well, oranges weren't on my mind at that time, but Mary was. And the logic of my thought went like this — women cause V.D., V.D. is very dangerous, with all those posters about pretty well everybody must have V.D.… Mary is an experienced girl and she's almost sure to have V.D. — Oh, my God, that means that I must have V.D., too.

"It was a week of absolute terror. I read the books, I devoured the pamphlets, I knew of by heart every symptom of every type of V.D. I developed a pimple on my nose and thought, hell, I've got secondary syphilis.

"Day by day, I looked at myself; I examined my body in the minutest detail. Nothing happened — day by day nothing at all happened. As reassurance developed confidence returned and with confidence curiosity surged… Mary was pretty interesting; Mary must be further investigated; Mary became a compelling interest.

"You know, it is a curious thing but, at this time, I could only attribute all these mysteries and fierce delights to Mary, and her alone. It did not really occur to me that other women might be the same. When it did cross my mind and I looked at other women, usually older, like the cashier or girls, I felt fantastically embarrassed and confused. I would redden and feel ashamed, almost to the point of apologising to them.

"Does familiarity breed contempt? For me, no — emphatically no. Every woman is still as great a mystery."

On, now, to the second incident — marriage. It came in a rush, and Harrison Marks explains how it happened:

"I never really had an adolescence. The war was a hot-house, almost overnight children became men and women this was a universal fact of the times. It happened most obviously in the Forces: it happened, too, in the factories. Life was fast, the pace accelerated all the time and somewhere, in the rush, the in-between time from childhood to being adult got lost.

"I was very much older than my years. At the film laboratories there was a woman, Diana. We grew very friendly. I liked to talk to her, and we seemed to get on well. She was a pleasant and friendly person.

"When my ulcers struck, I was on a tube train. I collapsed and was taken to hospital.

" 'It will take at least six weeks for you to recover,' they told me. What a place that was t It really frightened me. All round, all the time, people were dying. Every night the great, long mortuary trolley was wheeled in, and some poor bastard was wheeled out.

"At 17 this can have a profound effect on you. I began to think, 'That's the only way out of this place — and my turn's coming up!'

"After a fortnight I panicked. I telephoned Diana and demanded that she should pack up my clothes and get me out that very moment.

"In spite of the nurses, the sister, the matron and Diana, I voluntarily discharged myself. Diana insisted that I go home with her where she and her family could look after me.

"Five weeks later we were married. I pressurised my Mother into signing the papers. I was 17; she was 25.

"Like I said before, I really missed the guiding hand of my old man.

"But more about this later. Now, back to the music halls and the act we hadn't got, and our brass-necked cheek in putting ourselves before the Great British Public. Still, everybody has to start somewhere… even if it has to be at Walham Green.

CHAPTER 4

Six Years on the Halls

"IT wasn't that we were bad, just that we were as green as grass." That statement is not an excuse. It is a simple, undeniable statement of fact.

Music hall audiences tended to be meat eaters, red-blooded carnivores... not ruminants. So, perhaps, tongue-in-cheek, we can call this chapter: all the birds Harrison Marks never meant to get".

There is, in show-business, an axiom: "If you can't create — crib." For instance, bitterly Michael Bentine complains, "After just one television show, ten American comedians began using my drunken fly sketch." If anything, it is worse now than it ever was.

It works on the basis that if you do the act first at a new theatre or on a different television network or radio station, the audience is not to know it has been pinched, they might even think you are original.

Marks and Stuart cribbed. What else could they do? They borrowed a bit here and a bit there; they altered, they chopped and changed and threw in some original stuff, until they had an act.

Night and day they rehearsed, experimenting with make-up, practising songs. Generally as Harrison Marks says: "Flogging ourselves to death to polish it sufficiently to set before a real live audience."

And neither of them had ever seen a real live audience sitting in its plush red seats. Stupid, sullen and challenging all the time: "come on then, make me laugh".

It is, as Harrison Marks will ruefully tell you, a tough, tough game at which even the greatest have "died".

"Those few minutes, standing in the wings, waiting to go on at the Granville Theatre, Walham Green, were the most terrible in my life," Harrison Marks confesses. "It was the most awful experience I have ever had... ever. And I really mean that.

"I'm sure Sam felt the same. He looked GHASTLY. He looked worse than I felt. One last glance at him and he frightened me more than the audience.

"I was going to whisper 'Good Luck' or something. The trouble was I couldn't speak. I could not get one word out; my throat wouldn't work."

That is how they stepped into the glare of the footlights — the first faltering footsteps they hoped, to fame. Harrison Marks unable to give a single word of comfort or encouragement to Sam, who he knew full well was petrified with stage fright — and knowing full well, too that he himself was speechless.

The band struck up. They were on.

Harrison Marks: "It was different once we got on stage. We bounded out front and into the act and romped through it top speed. And I mean just that — we didn't stop once, regardless of who was laughing or not laughing and I should think our timing was about as lousy as it could be.

"As I said, it wasn't that we were bad — just as green as grass. For the difference between entertaining a gang of friends at a party and keeping a paying audience happy for eight minutes on stage is the difference between two worlds, and bridging the gap between the two can only be done with a lot of experience and heartache.

"During the time we were on the boards we learned to judge the mood of any audience in the land, to catch it, play with it, use it almost as if it was something we could hold in our hands — and that's what is known as being a professional.

"But at the beginning, we had to learn our lessons the hard way, just as everyone else did in those days when the live theatre flourished, before the days of 'instant talent' thrown up at us from television.

"I've known what it is to get the bird, or to sweat through an act that produced about as much response as a mating call in a cemetery. There were times when I wanted to quit, but found myself going back on because of the sheer magnetism of a profession that takes hold of you, deep down, and never quite lets you go. Even now, I can't stay away from the front of a camera when I'm making a picture.

"As they say, once a ham, always a ham.

"Sure, it was tough at first, but it was tough at first for better men than me — people like Alf Marks and Roy Castle, who did his apprenticeship with the great Jimmy James. They all had to go through it.

"I remember at the Grand, Brighton, Harry Secombe having a grim first house which would have depressed anyone else but him. Next time out, he took a big bundle of newspapers on stage with him and started throwing them at the audience. 'Well, folks,' he breezed. 'I'm here for six minutes… make yourselves comfortable. Have a read, and I'll get my bit over.'

"Yes, it was hard learning, but anyone who graduated in that school had what it takes, a professionalism and a talent that makes some of the telly-fodder and pop artists look like monkeys."

A tough business? Yes, but embracing some really marvellous people. Like Albert Rose, who used to run the Grand Theatre in Brighton, the man who gave me the first and only helping hand during my days there. Lots of people who are big now owe their breaks to Albert, and Norman Wisdom is one of them.

Albert Rose was a legend in the business. Foster father and mother, at one time or another, to pretty well everybody who has ever made it in Variety — he was the helping hand in a big way. Rose weaned more big acts to full-fledged stardom than almost anyone else in the business.

Memories are short and, sadly, when Variety collapsed under the impact of television and "flashin-the-pan" nude shows, not many cared to remember Albert. He hit very hard times. One man, however, never forgot and to the world-at-large he acted right out of character.

He was, at the time, Harrison Marks' idol, the "cheeky chappie" himself, Max Miller. "A comedian whose timing and command of an audience was sheer perfection and who was, in my book, the greatest.

"I know you can hear stories about him being a tightwad and all that, but they do him an injustice. I lived almost next door to Max in Brighton, and I knew him to be a quiet-living, easy-going fellow, and I had a lot of time for him as a man and as a performer. I think the mean bit grew up around him simply because he was not always prepared to buy drinks for all the hangers-on who kept coming up to him and slapping him on the back and giving the bit about how long it was since they had met.

"When you get to be a big name, it happens all the time, and it used to get under Max's skin.

"I've seen him tell that type of creep to fuck off and naturally they don't like it, but it always baffled me to know why people always expected him to buy drinks for the house just because he was Max Miller.

"And one thing I do know — Max was amongst those who tried to help Albert Rose when he hit hard times. And, as I said, very few others did.

"About the help bit, take the case of Norman Wisdom and Alf.

"I was there when Norman decided to quit show business for good and go back to where he came from and forget the whole bit. He had flogged himself to death with an act which was getting him no place at top speed and one day in Brighton he told Albert he was finishing.

" 'I'm wasting my time,' said Norman. 'Honestly, I don't think I'll ever make it.'

" 'Rubbish,' Albert said. 'All you need is a good act. Give me a week, and I'll figure something out, and we'll work at it until we've got it right. All right?'

" 'All right, if you think it's worth your time,' said Norman.

"And it was Albert who did most towards creating Norman's famous 'little man', and staked him until he got the act off pat. And when he had done that, he booked him. From there on, of course, Norman's career began to boom in a big way.

"Now, without any shadow of doubt, he's the biggest of his type everywhere in the world — look how he's wowed 'em in New York."

From the end of the war until it died so untimely a death early in the '50s, the variety stage encompassed two eras. There was a sharp, almost acute division between the "old troupers" who had been going since the turn of the century, and many from well before that, and the "new wave" of artists banging insistently at the door.

These were the people who, often, the war had thrown up. They came from different media and radio had boosted them.

In all they were in for a far tougher time than the old stagers. Radio was bad enough, but television was to come and hungrily devour their material at such a speed it often burned them out prematurely.

During the time of Harrison and Stuart, both eras shared the same bills, the new hustlers and the old pros — who had often been doing the same act for 50 years or more.

"I can remember Ella Shields coming to the theatre," Harrison Marks recalls. "A dear little woman shambling up to the stage door. So tiny, she looked as if she might blow away. Anybody's old, old grandmother. She must have been 70 then.

She'd lock herself in the dressing-room and half-an-hour later out she'd come. Somehow in that 30 minutes she had shed 40 years. I mean it, she had lost 40 years. Her face and figure were those of a woman of 30. She was taller and ramrod straight. You just couldn't see in her the tiny old lady who had arrived at the theatre. It was uncanny."

The whole scene comprised many more individuals; independent artists not fettered by great show business monopolies.

Men like Frank Randall. A disgusting old man to many people. Hated and a disastrous flop in the West End, but King, undisputed ruler of the North and Emperor of Blackpool for years.

"Randall had his own company which he ruled with a rod of iron — like he did the theatre managements. Life with him was, to say the least, uncertain.

"Everyone knows that he drank. So much that it would almost be an insult to a fish to compare them. I think it killed him eventually, poor chap.

"No one ever knew for certain whether he would be going on for a performance. It was sheer luck if he ever made it.

"Come to that, no one ever knew for certain if the show would go on. His company used to appear on a percentage of the house takings, with a guaranteed minimum.

"On one occasion, ten minutes before the curtain was due up, he demanded from the management, 'I'll have my £1,000 now, please.' It was absolutely unheard of. But Randall persisted, 1,000 NOW or NO show '

"The management explained that they just hadn't got the money in the house — he could have it as soon as the banks opened in the morning. 'No money,' Randall was adamant, 'NO SHOW'… that was it, the show was cancelled, the audience got its cash back."

The funniest thing Harrison Marks can recall about Randall happened in London.

"It was Saturday night at the old Chiswick Empire, and poor old Frank was blind, stoned out of his mind. 'I can't go on,' he kept saying 'I can't go on, I'm too ill.'

"So Gus Allbury, a sweet character, who was Frank's stooge and understudy, had to take the part.

"The audience were a bit restive, they'd paid to see Randall, and they wanted him. They definitely expected him on in the second half.

"The second half started and he was still too 'ill' to appear. Then suddenly, right in the middle of the big comic sketch, he walked on without his comedy make up and in his normal street clothes.

" 'Stop,' he commanded. Then he climbed into the orchestra pit, 'you can go home,' he told the conductor. He shouted to Allbury 'Get all the company on stage.'

"Of course, the company were used to him — and all sorts of odd things happening. They rushed on and lined up.

" 'Right,' said Randall, 'now we'll have the Hallelujah Chorus… One, two, three… Hallelujah.' They went all the way through it."

Randall wasn't the only boozer Harrison Marks recalls.

"There was Tod Slaughter. For years he'd toured in 'Sweeny Todd, the demon barber of Fleet Street' and that other blood-curdler, Jack-the-Ripper.

"It was when he was playing Jack-the-Ripper. The last scene is his big soliloquy, he's on stage completely alone and spelling out his thoughts — all great ham stuff.

"This night, some idiot let him off the leash between acts, in a flash, he was over the road in the boozer and tippling it back. Comes his cue and there's no Tod.

"So the company ad-libs while a search party is sent out — they were used to it too.

"The search party didn't have to look far. He was rushed back and poured onto the stage. All wild-eyed and shattered — very dramatic.

"The cast melted into the wings, and he started his big speech.

"The only thing was that he started to spout King Lear. For seven full minutes he carried on doing Lear. They had to wait till he came near the wings and one of the cast hissed: 'you should be doing Jack-the-Ripper, not Lear.

"Slaughter stared. It all looked like part of the business. 'Oh,' he muttered, and went straight into Jack.

"All that happened was that the curtain was seven minutes late. The audience never even noticed — they didn't utter a murmur."

Really there is precious little glamour in show business. You spend your life waiting to shine for eight to twelve minutes a night, occasionally at an afternoon matinee. Eight minutes a night, six nights a week and Sunday is a day of travel to the next theatre. And Sunday is the day the railways go haywire. It is indeed a tough life. Probably the toughest part being how to fill in the 23 hours 52 minutes between the act. Particularly when you are in a really dead-and-alive town out in the sticks. You don't know anybody. Nowhere is open, few people want to know you. Understandably, digs assume a great importance.

There are good digs, bad digs, indescribable digs — all have to be put up with but little things can put you off.

"We arrived in Hull one night," says Harrison Marks. "The digs were highly recommended and they really were good. Very comfortable. Immediately our spirits soared, 'We're in for a good week,' I said to Sam.

— Don't be late for dinner,' the landlady said in a rich northern voice. 'We all 'ave us dinner together at 8 o'clock.'

"There was a big table, all the guests were seated round, it was rather like Aunt Esther's. We hadn't eaten all day, and boy, was that soup good. The meat came up and it looked and smelled a real treat.

"The dear old landlady asked: "ave you all got enough meat then? Sure? Very well, I'll get the vegetables. There was a clatter in the kitchen; the smells were even more appetising.

"I smiled and winked at Stuart — then the smile froze on my lips. The beaming landlady had reappeared. In her left hand she carried, filled to the brim with lush green peas — an enamel utensil; in the right hand, filled to overflowing with roast potatoes a second enamel utensil. That's right, I mean piss-pots. 'Don't mind the pots, luv, will you,' she smiled. 'They're very much cheaper than baking dishes — and so much stronger!'

" 'Oh,' she added with a little giggle and a reassuring smile, 'we don't use them for *anything* else, oh dear me no.'

"We couldn't eat another thing in the house all week. We lived the rest of the time on fish and chips.

"Being Hull, the fish was very fresh."

It was tiring, exacting, demanding work, but this was how friends were made. Sooner or later you were bound to meet up with everybody 'on the circuit.'

Today, although Harrison Marks' activities are more concerned with films, old friendships remain firm. When he was making his first full-length slap-stick comedy "The Chimney Sweeps," he was able to recruit half a dozen of his old colleagues from Variety to play with him in it.

Socially he surrounds himself with people from the live theatre rather than with film associates. His home is "open house" most evenings of the week, and his dinner table usually reads like a show business who's who. Conversation is most times about "the business" and over glasses of brandy, gags, reminiscences and opinions are exchanged until the first light of day appears in the sky.

The sheer professionalism of the old stagers fascinates Harrison Marks.

He talks about G. H. Elliott: "A perfect and refined gentleman. So gentle and immaculate. He'd been doing the act for 60 years and he was still great.

"You know, in his dressing room there were always twelve immaculate white suits and twelve shirts and on the wall there hung a notice. 'Mr. Elliott requests that you kindly do not smoke because it affects his throat — thank you."

Another was Billy Russell.

"It took me nine months before I saw him as he really was. You couldn't possibly recognise him off stage. And what a surprise. Instead of the big, red-nosed comic, here was a quiet man with gentle classical features.

"Every performance, he took two hours to put on that make-up. Two solid hours for a twelve-minute performance. That was the care those old timers took."

Later Harrison Marks was to get a big surprise from Russell. "It's a technical thing," he says, "a little point, but it shook me.

"On Billy's arm during the act was a fabulous, gaudy tattoo of a naked woman. It stretched from elbow to wrist.

"When I'd left the business, he came to my studio to be photographed.

"Again, it took him two hours to make-up. Suddenly I looked at him and asked in surprise, 'Where's the tattoo?'

" 'Oh, I always put that on last,' he said.

"I was astonished. It was a work of art. It looked as if it had taken days to do. Yet, every working day for 50 years or so he'd drawn that thing on.

"That wasn't the only thing about Billy that surprised me.

"When I was in Manchester, I got into an argument about him. Somebody had said, 'Billy Russell, the greatest Lancashire comedian of the lot.'

"Don't be silly, I replied, he's a cockney comic, and the argument started.

"Next time I saw him, I said, 'Hey, Bill, some idiot was trying to tell me the other day that you were a Lancashire comedian.'

" 'That's right,' he said, 'when I'm up there, I play the act in a northern accent, like when I'm in Scotland I play it in Glaswegian… and in Wales I go Welsh.'

"And every accent was perfect."

Kind people they were, Harrison Marks remembers, kind and generous. There was a great comradeship on the road.

"Like poor old Jimmy James, the best, the funniest drunk act there has ever been… and he was a strict teetotaller.

"He died almost broke. He was good for any tap. Anyone who had been in the business was sure of a good thing if he tapped Jimmy.

"He never touched a drop, but he never missed a bet on a horse or a dog. That was his big weakness.

Of all heterogeneous groups, Music Hall artists rate pretty high as story tellers and reminiscencers; they must rank only with old soldiers in remembering the good times and obliterating the dull, awful weeks, months and years separating the highlights. Talk comes easily and freely but more in the vein of those who have survived an ordeal rather than won a victory. In truth it was the dreariest of lives: an existence of no fixed address, no real roots, monotonous and tedious.

It was in Hull that Harrison and Stuart decided to quit. In the middle of one week, without any previous discussion simultaneously they decided that they had had enough. In six years they had witnessed the mercurial ups and downs, the riches and rags of the business.

By and large, the money was good. It could be exceptional. Harrison Marks had worked with one act which started from nothing and rocketed to the top in a matter of weeks.

This was Jack Wafer, who did a hypnotic act, who was particularly well known in the North.

Harrison Marks tells his story: "Jack had arrived in this country straight from Ireland. He was a really glib-tongued Irishman with the blarney and the gift of the gab. In short, he could convince almost anybody of anything.

"He desperately wanted to get into show business and he decided to try hypnotism, which was all the rage at the time. The top hypnotist, Ralph Slater, was at the Palladium earning £2,000 a week.

"Not to put too fine a point on it, Jack watched Slater's act over and over again — and modelled himself entirely on Slater — actions, patter, everything. Then he sold himself to an agent on the lines that he had just arrived from America.

"He surprisingly got a booking for a week… bear in mind that he didn't know a damned thing about hypnotism, except what he had seen Slater do."

Harrison Marks looks at hypnotism with a strictly professional eye.

"Of course, all stage hypnotism is basically autosuggestion, the audience is preconditioned into doing what the hypnotist wants. Wafer, who had never been on a stage before, went over really big, immediately in his first week.

"In a month, he was billed as a star, earning £ 800 a week… and spending it. I promise you, I have seen that man put two-thirds of an audience of 2,000 under the spell.

"In Nottingham, he had the chief of police suspended rigid between two stands, his head on one, and his feet on the other with Jack jumping up and down on his stomach.

"And remember, Jack knew damn all about hypnotism either as a science or as an art.

"But it is all codology, take this case: We were at a cocktail party once and he was surrounded by a bunch of young girls. They were all chattering away to him; 'Hypnotise me, Mr. Wafer,' or bet you can't hypnotise me, Mr. Wafer.'

"That usually means they're a dead ringer for it anyway.

"Suddenly Jack called me and told the girls: 'This is Professor Markison, one of the greatest hypnotists from America. Come on professor,' he said, 'put one of the girls under.'

"So I acted up. I thought they all realised it was a gag, and that I was really the comic in the show. I fixed a tall brunette with a piercing stare, 'look at me, look me in the eyes, when I tell you to go to sleep, you will go to sleep.' I gave her all the patter, but sending it up with a phoney voice. Then I jabbed a finger at her and yelled: 'Go to sleep.'

"I turned to the bar to pick up my drink and there was a great thump. I spun round and there she was flat out stiff as a poker on her back on the floor — out cold. She'd gone down like she was pole-axed.

"Sometime later, I quit the business and the next time I saw Jack was in Brighton when I had set up as a theatrical photographer. He was stoney broke — so was I. We couldn't even raise 1½d. for the bus fare to the station.

CHAPTER 5

London and Life in a Brothel

EVERYTHING was fine in Brighton when Harrison Marks returned to photography. The town supported three live theatres, just enough in turn to support a theatrical photographer. And London was near enough for the odd job.

Occasionally the going was a little tough. During one of these periods in the winter, a friend of Harrison Marks, who managed a chain store in the town, telephoned him with a proposition which sounded promising. The store was setting up a Christmas Grotto. Would Harrison Marks take pictures of the children talking to Father Christmas: the terms 30 per cent to the shop, 70 per cent to him.

Times were slack and it wasn't *quite* his cup of tea. Nevertheless, he called his old pal Jimmy MacNeil the Oxford Street photographer who had moved to Worthing. Winter was quiet for him too. So they teamed up again.

"It sounded a push-over, and we turned up at the store the following Monday full of high hopes and Christmas cheer. But our expectations dipped a bit when we saw Father Christmas — you never saw a more miserable-looking old devil in your life.

"Far from enticing the little boys and girls, it looked more likely that he'd put the fear of God into them, sitting there with an expression of doom that made a mockery of his white whiskers and fine red robe.

"Jimmy's jaw dropped when he saw him. 'Christ,' he whispered, 'he looks more like Boris Karloff than Santa Claus.' Even when Jimmy went over to chat the old boy up and try to put a smile on his face, he only mumbled something in his beard and relapsed into gloom. That morning was a disaster. The kids who did go into the grotto shied away from Santa and this worried me. The old boy was my meal ticket and I decided we had better do something, so after a couple of hours, I gave Jimmy the wink and we slid away to the pub down the street.

"It was obvious that we were going to have to have a serious talk with Santa, and the quicker the better. So we scuttled back to the store and I went up and whispered to him. 'Come out for a drink, Dad.' This brought the tiniest flash of interest to his face, but he rapidly killed that and said he couldn't leave and go out in his get-up. However, I eventually talked him into slipping his overcoat around his shoulders and coming down to the pub for a drink and a chat. And thinking I'd get things on the right footing, I ordered up a double Scotch for him.

"Well, every man has his weakness and Scotch was obviously Santa's vice, for he put that double away with a speed and smoothness that would have earned the respect of any Scotsman. What's more he actually smiled.

"I got him another and after downing that, he started to chuckle. A third double had him laughing and after one more, he was ready to dance.

"I glanced at Mac. 'This is the answer,' I said. And, by Heaven, it was. Back on his throne in the grotto, Father Christmas was a changed man. He rocked with laughter, called out to the kids, back-chatted the Mums and snatched up a set of hand-bells and began ringing them until every eye in the store was on him. Soon, the children were flocking to him, Mac was working his fingers off taking their pictures and I was playing a non-stop tune on the cash register. A couple more drinks at lunchtime kept Santa in the mood and we ended the day with a fair old take.

"The following morning, the old boy had returned to his former deep depression but this time Mac and I had come prepared with a bottle. At the back of the grotto the three of us had a quick couple of slugs which was enough to put Santa back in form, so we wheeled him out to his throne and left the rest to him.

"That job cost Mac and I two bottles of Scotch a day but it was well worth it, for as long as Father Christmas kept laughing, we were filling our stocking. But perhaps it was just as well that none of the grown-ups got near enough to smell his breath!

We kept him permanently stoned from 9.30 every morning through until closing time from the Tuesday until Christmas Eve.

"The drunker he was the better. If business slackened, we would pour him a stiff shot and say, 'come on, Dad, drum 'em in.'

"He would bound up the stairs out into the street, ringing his handbell and sounding like a convoy of fire engines. Then he'd come back with half the kids of Brighton on his tail.

"Meanwhile, my cash register was ringing louder and faster than his handbells.

Only the public's stupidity allows a Grafter to operate, and the public are very funny. Mac was prancing round Father Christmas, snapping the kiddywinks and chatting up the Mums. With the soppiest looks, mothers watched their little horrors telling Santa what they wanted. They were so softened up, that they were a pushover and Mac would chip in, 'isn't she (he) lovely, it's marvellous how they look when they meet Santa — if you would like a picture just leave your name and address at the desk.

" 'Lovely,' most of the Mums would say, 'thank you.' Until then no price had been mentioned and the Mums were so besotted that they probably thought they were free. I soon disillusioned them. With a sweet smile I'd say: 'How many would you like? Go on, have six.' And most would reply incredulously, Can I?'

" 'Course you can, dear. Now give me your name and address.' Then deliberately, I would write it down and read it back… Mrs. J. Smith, 16 so and so… The funny thing is that there seems to be some magic about giving your name and address. It is probably a throwback to childhood days when there was the threat that the policeman would take your name and address. Anyway, once people have given it they seldom argue. Odd, isn't it? Then quietly and quickly, I'd hand over the receipt… 10s. 6d. please. There was usually a momentary flutter. 'Oh,' the lady would say.

But the 10s. 6d. came over. A big, flashing smile from me and off they went happy as larks.

"The odd one would question, 'I thought it was free?'

" 'Well, it is really, dear. This is only to cover the cost of printing, packaging and post; we don't charge for the photographer or the service.'

"A blank look, 'Oh,' and the 10s. 6d. came rattling across."

So merry as the jingle of sleigh bells across the snow the case of the intoxicated Father Christmas continued until realisation dawned upon Harrison Marks. He checked the till and with a shocked exclamation he told Mac: "At this rate we'll be paying this lot (the store) £100 a week for this pitch!"

" 'Outrageous,' said Mac, genuinely staggered. 'It's chucking good money down the drain.'

" 'After all, we're subsidising them with Scotch,' he reasoned. He was very upset.

The habits of private enterprise and self-unemployment die hard. And there is always tomorrow to be considered.

"So I got it on a more equitable basis," Harrison Marks says, "two for me, one for the cash register. I had to be a bit smartish, though, and keep a wide eye for the floor manager, shop walkers and store detectives. It was all right, as a matter of fact, when we cashed in the store people were delighted. It was a fantastic success. I carried on with my slight touch of the Houdinis with the ten and sixpences."

Nothing is really worthwhile if it comes too easy and success is meaningless unless obstacles have been overcome to attain it. They trundled Santa back from his liquid lunch one day and met the big obstacle. A charming and pretty seventeenyear-old girl and a big bin accompanied by the floor manager.

"We completely forgot about the lucky dip," said the floor manager, "and the only possible place we can put it is next to your desk. It'll be a little cramped, but I'm sure you won't mind, will you?"

"How could we," says Harrison Marks, "it was his shop."

Mac's face fell and George's ready smile was a little fixed. The girl was sitting right next to George on the desk and next to the cash register.

"That's the fiddle up the spout," he thought. "I haven't got the room to work my left arm. '

The full seriousness of the situation was becoming more and more apparent. Slowly Mac turned, "George boy," he said, very quietly and almost menacingly, "George, you have a penchant for the ladies, you have a knack with them which is the envy of half the boys in the town. Now you'll have to use it, you'll have to put in some overtime. Now don't argue, Georgie, lad. It's only fair, I keep old Santa happy all day, I keep lifting him back on his stool all day when he looks like falling off. And I have to keep feeding him slugs all day, and keeping him company. I wake up every morning with a terrible hangover just from keeping him happy. Now it's your turn. Come on, fifty-fifty."

"Thank God she was pretty," Harrison Marks says. She had to be won over.

"By half-past three, she was well hooked. By the following morning she was madly in love. I tried the old hypnotic touch, staring intently into her eyes… and she stared back. Never once did she watch the till. I was doing my left-hand bit down by her legs and she thought I was giving her a bit of a tickle-up.

"I was the most considerate lover. 'Go on, love,' I'd tell her, 'nip up for a cup of tea. I'll watch the bin and I'll say you've popped to the ladies room if anyone asks.

"Have a dip," I'd tell the customers. "Half-a dollar." I wound up taking a couple of quid a day out of the dip as well."

Merry Christmas came and went. So did the cash. Again things were getting pushed.

One morning the bell rang at the flat in Brunswick Square. It was Jack Wafer, the hypnotist, flat broke and shabby. Hypnotic acts were dead, the £800 a week had dwindled to nothing and unfortunately things in the Harrison Marks household were just as thin.

You cannot keep an ebullient Irishman down for long, however, and Mr. Wafer, as ever, was full of ideas.

Meanwhile, he had one booking, to play an American camp for a week for £60. How like the old song:

"The Vanderbilts have asked us up for tea,
We don't know how to get there, no siree."

The U.S.O. have asked him to the club, but how's he going to get there that's the rub.

Nine a.m. prompt on Monday morning, the camp coach was due to leave Victoria, in London. By turning out the drawers and ornaments, tapping the neighbours for a couple of shillings — "the gas has gone out, and I haven't any change" — and including farthings, they rustled up the travel money. All but 1½d., they were short of this for the bus fare to Brighton Station. Jack Wafer left at 5.30 a.m. to walk, but he made it in a suit and overcoat borrowed from Harrison Marks.

Mr. Wafer was to be around for some time and it was never dull. Back in the Brunswick Square digs, he announced one day: "I'm going to be a comic."

"Oh give over, do me a favour," said Harrison Marks.

"No," Jack insisted, "I've watched Jack Durante (the American comedian) and I know I can do that act."

So he styled himself on Durante. Albert Rose, the philanthropic Albert, booked him for a week at £30 "for old times sake."

The next three weeks were hell while Jack rehearsed. He played the whole act as if he were still a hypnotist. His timing was terrible. With a hoot of triumph, he produced, one day, a trumpet mouthpiece — no trumpet, just the mouthpiece which a musician at the theatre had loaned him.

"It's only the lipping," he explained. "That's the secret. I'm going to do a big trumpet solo as the finale to my act."

Harrison Marks' protests that he had never played a trumpet in his life, were brushed aside.

"I've told you," Jack insisted, its just the lipping, it's easy — the band can easily busk the rest."

"For the next few days," says Harrison Marks, he wandered round the flat making the most excruciating, vulgar noises. The place sounded like an overworked public convenience. The neighbours started giving me curious looks. It was terrible."

The kind-hearted Albert Rose telephoned Bernard Luper, the tailor to fit Jack out with a dress suit. He paid for it out of his own pocket.

Came Monday night. For the first time in his life Jack collected a complete trumpet. An hour before the curtain he was in a state of nerves. Two large whiskies brought back his confidence. "I'll wow 'em when I get out there; they'll love it."

Harrison Marks went out front. "To be fair, utterly fair," he says, "I have never seen a more disastrous act. It was murder. He mixed his lines, he got flustered. Sure, he was word perfect but all in the wrong places. He played the whole act in a monotone with absolutely no timing — every gag misfired. You couldn't tell they were meant to be gags. Then came the trumpet bit. He called for the instrument from the orchestra, put it to his lips and three frantic screeches pierced the air, each one wilder than the last. The stage manager couldn't stand it. He dropped the tabs on him."

Albert Rose stood at the back of the stalls, hunched and trying to look even tinier, he was only five foot three inches anyway. His head was buried in his hands all the way through the act.

Slowly, they went back stage. "Cut out the trumpet part," said Albert, weakly.

No stopping Mr. Wafer. "I was only nervous, Albert," he said, "I'll be all right next house — I'll wow em.

Eventually, Albert said, "Jack, do yourself a good turn, just walk on and introduce the other turns. No comedy, please, no comedy — and for Christ's sake — no trumpet "

Failure merely stimulated the redoubtable Mr. Wafer. His next stunt was to be Jekyll and Hyde. He got the idea when he had a raging toothache and the dentist gave him some tablets.

Clearly, he was allergic to them; his face swelled to enormous proportions almost as soon as he took them.

"He was so glib, he talked me into believing it," said Harrison Marks. "It looked so effective, eventually, I offered to be his manager." The drawback was that he grew used to them, the tablets didn't work successfully every time.

As ever, convinced that it "would be all right on the night," Jack summoned the press to see his new, sensational act.

He gulped down the tablets, a double dose. Nothing happened. Mr. Jekyll, and his manager, just wanted to hide.

"Let me tell you about the time he really scared me," says Harrison Marks. "Somewhere he had picked up a cheap fairground gadget. It was a fearsome looking electrical machine. Dozens of impressive coils and tubes — most of them codology, I suppose. But when you switched it on a great flash of blue lightning leapt across two points about three feet' apart. It made the devil of a din. It was quite alarming.

" 'My new act,' said Jack proudly: 'Jack Wafer, the human lightning conductor, the man who defies nature and the power of the elements.'

"I told him he was mad.

"He stood in front of the contraption, switched it on, this great flash of lightning jumped right up his fingers. And there he was with two crackling streaks flashing out of both hands.

"Stop it," I screamed.

" 'It's O.K.,' he said, quite hurt. 'I'm wearing rubber socks.'

"But what happens if you get a hole in your sock or there's moisture in the air?'

" 'I'll get fried,' he replied.

"We short-circuited that idea very smartish."

Jack didn't fry, instead he nearly starved to death, deliberately. The papers carried a report that a man in Palermo, Italy, had broken the world's starvation record. Just the sort of idiocy to appeal to Mr. Wafer.

Quickly he found himself a sponsor. A shop window was rigged out with a bed and a screen which he could pop behind now and again when nature called. It was, in effect, a glass cage, his sole communication with the world was a telephone.

A big screen was placed in front of the window and for one shilling a go, day or night, the public were invited to watch him starve.

And starve he did. For weeks and weeks and weeks he lived solely on soda water, which was in fact, allowed in the contest. He starved until he resembled a Belsen victim and the public rolled up by the dozens to witness the whole sordid spectacle. He broke the world record and collected a miserable few hundred pounds for very nearly wrecking his health. It took months for his system to return to normal. The public, in its infinite wisdom, loves a spectacle no matter how degrading and Mr. Wafer's fame had spread so far that he received an offer from Barnum and Bailey to stage the same act in the circus in New York.

He was to travel across to America in the Queen Mary, lying night and day in a glass coffin and living again on soda water. Publicity was laid on to cover the departure and arrival in the States. It was all going to be really a piece of hookum and the faster Mr. Wafer grew thinner, the quicker he would grow richer. The day before he was due to sail, he caught German measles. The kindest thing that could possibly have happened.

For the record, these are the facts.

At three minutes past six in the evening of Monday, October 6, 1952, Wafer broke the world fasting record of 72 days, three hours, three minutes set up by Burmah, an Indian Fakir, in Palermo, in Italy.

Wafer went into his glass cage in Queen's Road, Brighton, on July 26, and he stayed in it all together for 76 days, in spite of the pleas of his wife.

Most newspaper reports agree that he drank 500 bottles of soda water and smoked 2,500 cigarettes during the time he lived in his lift. by 7ft. glass cage.

Not many of the reports were enthusiastic. One said he was exposing himself to public curiosity and contempt. Many questioned the validity of the experiment.

It was said originally that he had undertaken the fast in a bid to win £8,000 offered by an American millionaire and a Belgian gourmet. It is doubtful if Wafer collected a tenth of that amount.

His second attempt at a long fast in December of the same year ended with measles. It was to have been an endurance contest with a German, Willi Schmitz, and another Indian Fakir, Reikan.

For this attempt, Wafer was sealed in his glass case and exhibited at the funfair at Olympia circus. Then the idea was to transport him — coffin and all — across to New York.

Brighton came to an end because of an outbreak of Smallpox. The three theatres were closed.

Nothing at all was happening and the Harrison Marks fortune had declined to the classical 1s. 4d. Desperation stakes. "I had flogged bits of equipment and pawned others and lived on a diet of chips and Woodbines. The bloke who collected the rent began to mutter nasty things and it got to the stage when I was scared to answer a knock on the door. I had got past the stage of jumping when the phone rang — they'd cut that off! In al I suppose I owed about a hundred quid, and it's a funny thing about when you owe a little amount, people won't let you alone. If you owe fifty thousand, they're afraid to come near you. Anyway, the last straw was when the local newsagent came banging on the door for his bill — all eighteen shillings of it. It just broke my heart.

"Apart from that, I had my Alsatian dog to think about. In the end, I decided there was only one way of getting out from under. I'd do a moonlight flit! It was a desperate move, but I *was* desperate. I rang up a pal of mine who had a haulage business between Brighton and London and asked if he'd take the dog and me up to town that night. So it was that I slipped out of the house shortly after midnight and crept away from Brighton, my overdraft, the newsagent and all the other creditors.

"We arrived at Marble Arch at about four o'clock on a bitterly cold morning. Arthur, the haulage contractor, good bloke that he was, asked me if I was all right for the ready stuff but for the life of me I could not take anything from him. He had brought me up to London for nothing and I simply couldn't tap him for a quid on top. So I put on a big smile and said sure, I was all right thank you and off he went.

"It was then I did a quick count-up of my resources. And it was damned quick, too! All I had were two tanners, four pennies and a halfpenny. Plus, of course, the dog and a suitcase with a suit and a couple of shirts in it.

"I can tell you that I have never felt so low in my life. I had absolutely nothing. No job, nowhere to kip, no prospects and next to no money. All I could think of to do was to walk down Oxford Street to Lyons Corner House at Tottenham Court Road and lash out on a cup of tea. It was somewhere at least to sit and think.

"So the dog and I set off and arrived in Joe's at about five. I spent fourpence on a cup of tea — which I shared with the dog — and sat there. But, far from gathering inspiration, my mind just went blank. All I could think was that in about two hours London was going to come alive and I'd have to move on. But where to?

"But fate is a funny thing. And it was pure fate which saved me that night. For across the room, I noticed a familiar face. I couldn't quite place it, but it belonged to a chap I had once known and, thank God, he remembered me and came across to sit at my table.

"Well, I was so relieved to find a friendly face, I just poured out the whole tale.

"His name? We'll come to that later.

"When I'd said my piece this bloke suddenly threw out an offer which saved my life.

" 'I've got an attic in my house in Charlotte Street… you can have it if you like until you get on your feet.' I could have kissed him; I was so grateful. I didn't though, but went round with him to his house and up to the attic.

"Well, he said it wasn't much of a room — and boy, he was right You never saw such a mess. It was about as big as a coffin and half as inviting. There was an old dressing table and a rusty iron bed — no mattress, just a bed — and a gas bracket hanging off the wall. And that was that. Still, it was somewhere for the dog to kip. And I was so tired and depressed I accepted with thanks.

"Anyway, he put a mattress on the bed and I crashed out on it with the dog on the floor. I must say I began to wish I'd put the dog in the bed after about five minutes, though. That mattress needed chains to keep it on the bed; it was so lousy, but it is a measure of how tired I was that I slept on it like a babe.

"I was woken about mid-day by the sound of the dog barking and I sat up to find out what he was growling at. I thought there was a hell of a lot of coming and going in the house and even when I went down to the basement — where the man lived — and passed half a dozen men on the stairs; I didn't realise…

"In fact, I was living there for two days before I tumbled — the place was a brothel!

"His name? you ask. Well, let's forget, never Welsh on a true friend."

Swinging London. There they were in this house of ill repute, the down and out, the dog and the dollies. All in utter squalor, but unknowingly, for the down and out at least, a step, faltering though it may have been, away from success. The Harrison Marks story continues:

"I must say one thing. I found out that some prostitutes really do have hearts of gold. I never patronised them but I used to talk to them a lot and, you know, they were marvellous types, always ready to help, inviting me in for tea and so on. I had a lot of time for them. One lent me £8 to get a camera out of pawn.

"It was in this knocking shop that I set up my first London darkrooms, in a washroom at the back of the basement, and started the rounds of the showbiz agents in town, touting for photographic work.

"But work, any kind of work, was imperative. There were jobs by the score to be had, at this time staff was almost impossible to find. I'm convinced that is the only reason why I got into the mail-order business.

"A small dress manufacturer put an advertisement in the *Evening Standard* for an office manager. It turned out that he had a couple of very good gown shops in Manchester and another in Liverpool, plus a factory. His dresses were, in fact, very good quality.

"At this time he was gearing up for a mail order campaign — though campaign is hardly the right word. What, in fact, was happening is that he was putting one advertisement in the News of the World for a dress, three sizes, three colours — 39s. 11d. delivered by return of post. Simple?

"Well not quite so simple as it seems. Advertising space in the News of the World in those days was like gold-dust. The first hurdle was to get the space and the far steeper hurdle was to pass the News of the World vetting. In this mail-order business, the newspaper examines the prospective advertiser almost through a microscope. The reason is obviously that they are anxious to prevent their readers being cheated and to protect their own good name.

"They want to see the factory, the goods, the facilities and every detail almost to asking for the advertiser's grandmother's birth certificate.

"My boss had an excellent factory, he also had some pull, for he managed to convince the paper he could cope, which he, and I, thought he could.

"Staff was so short and he was so desperate that he agreed to all my terms. I blush at my own damned cheek, and I hadn't got a penny, yet I insisted that I would be allowed half-days off to seek photographic work, telephone calls in and out and that the dog should be allowed in the office.

"He agreed.

"I knew nothing about the mail order business and, really, I couldn't have cared less. For me, it was to be strictly a small-time operation.

"In the first week, I got the office organised, strictly for my own convenience. If any theatrical agents called, the girls were instructed to take messages and the office joke became that every time the phone rang I made a corny quip: 'If that's Bernard Delfont, tell him I'm busy.'

"In my spare time, I nipped round to see Harry Kweller, a small printer in Soho, and got him to run me off 50 visiting cards with just my name and the office number on them, which I spread round the agencies. The agents assumed that this was my studio number and the girls who answered were my staff.

"Basically my job at the mail order office was to arrange for the despatch of the goods when the orders arrived after the envelopes had been opened.

" 'We should clear a few thousand dresses,' my boss said. We did — and how. The Tuesday after the ad. appeared the postman came.

"The postman always knocks twice, they say. This one didn't, he hammered ten times, with ten G.P.O. sacks of mail. Now, a G.P.O. mailbag is about four-foot-six high and almost as wide. It holds an awful lot of letters. That was the beginning. Every subsequent post, and there were three deliveries a day, brought on average, nine more sacks.

"The office was more than knee-deep in letters. It was difficult to get in. Two-pound postal orders were lying everywhere. Scrunch, scrunch, scrunch, we were walking on a carpet of loot. It appeared impossible to cope with this fantastic avalanche of orders.

"On the second day the boss broke down. He paced up and down the showroom, head in hands. 'What are we going to do, George, whatever are we going to do,' he wailed over and over again.

"Frankly, I felt much the same, but money has always had a galvanising effect on my metabolism. At the sight of it the adrenaline pours into my blood-stream. I rise to dizzy peaks of brilliance.

"I took command. 'Get organised,' I said with astonishing firmness. 'Let's be sensible about it. You know all about dresses and ordering them and how to get the factory to produce the right numbers in the right colour at the right size,

"You do the dresses… I'll count the money," I instructed.

Well, reader, you may have guessed by now what happened. But desperate situations demand desperate remedies and Harrison Marks has never pretended to be a cardboard saint, or a saint of any calibre for that matter.

"All right, I confess," he says, "I screwed the old boy, and this is how. The ad stated clearly: send postal order for £ 2 2s. 9d. made out to so-and-so gowns (dept. N.W.) crossed & Co.

"You would be surprised, if shocked, at the number of innocents who send completely blank P.O.'s — no name, no nothing, just blank. I was surprised, very, very pleasantly surprised.

"I marked the coupons 'paid' and decided on an equitable share out. Two or three for him, the odd blank one for me.

"He was happy. Slowly, the colour crept back into his cheeks and a smile again began to crease his lips. His bank manager began to rush to open the door for him when he made his daily, sometimes twice daily, calls.

"Vunderful; he kept whispering.

"Vunderful, it's a miracle,' and he cracked a little joke. 'I'm getting rich so fast I don't know if I'm on my ass or my elbow.'

"I didn't say 'snap' and I couldn't care much about his 'ass or his elbow,' all I knew was that I was getting on my feet again.

"How we worked, 12 to 16 hours a day. 'George,' he kept saying, 'You're a wonderful willing boy, stick with me and you've got a big future.'

"All the time the phone kept ringing. Our spirits were as high as they could be. Every time it ran I sang out: 'If that's Delfont, tell him I'm too busy counting loot to talk to him, I'll call him back.

" 'George,' said the little switch-girl, one day, le says it is Bernard Delfont.'

"Oh, give me the phone," I snapped, certain that it was a joke. "What's all this, I bellowed into the mouthpiece.

"A voice at the other end replied, 'This is Bernard Delfont, Norman Wisdom has just shown me some pictures you took of him in Brighton. I like them. I'd like you to come and see me.'

" 'Yes, Mr. Bernard er… I mean… Mr. Delfont,' I said very softly, 'I'll be round in half an hour."

CHAPTER 6

My Mistress Lady X

LUCKY Leo's. No matter how hard the going, something turns up for them. Sooner or later the sun shines, they are the born extroverts, the leaders… the lovers.

"There were diversions and, I make no bones about it, most of mine have been with women. This one was no exception — with one qualification. Usually I have showered my girlfriends with presents, this time, it was quite the reverse.

"The lady in question was a widowed lady, titled and right out of the top drawer in society. In the study of her home were signed photographs of princes and princesses and Royal Dukes and a fine portrait of that fine old lady, Queen Mary. Yes, it was as high as that. All the photographs were autographed affectionately, as one would naturally sign a picture for a close friend or relative.

"I am, I consider a rich man now. If I worked until I was 100, I could never be as wealthy as this lady. Basically all was set for a monumental, memorable affair. That is just what happened.

"You can never tell when these things will hit you, particularly when you fall in love as easily as I do. I had been spending a lot of time at the Irving Theatre Club; she was a member, too.

"When we first met, she was no more, to me, than a rather arty oddball. She used to wear tweed suits, her hair in a bun and a monocle. I had not caught her name when we had been introduced, but she had said she wanted some pictures taken and I had given her my card and thought no more about it.

"Two days after that, she rang up. I was very surprised to learn she had a title, but I looked on her as no more than a twenty-guinea job and I agreed to go round to her home — in Belgravia — and take some portraits.

"I rolled up to this expensive address in a taxi, complete with cameras, tripods, floodlights and all, dressed in my old green corduroy suit, looking like everyone's idea of a rather intellectual photographer.

"I couldn't find the bell — it's more difficult than you think at those big houses — so I bailed on the door and was greeted by Her Ladyship's man.

"The butler conducted me to the library. Conducted is the only word. That chap had style; he looked the type who would never dream of throwing me out, he would send for the under-footman to do it. I was glad to reach the library.

"And there, I got my second shock of the day. I found that Lady X, with her hair down, was really a very attractive woman. She welcomed me cordially and we talked for a bit about this and that and then I got down to taking her pictures. The session lasted a couple of hours, I suppose, at the end of which the room was extremely hot. I was very glad when she suggested we went upstairs to her drawing room for a drink.

" 'Pour me a gin and tonic,' she said. 'I shan't be a minute. I'm just going to get changed.

"I helped myself to a drink, sat down and waited for her. Two minutes later, the door opened — and I nearly fell off my chair with shock

"Lady X wafted into the room wearing a flimsy housecoat and a warm smile. That was all I

"Even then, I couldn't believe that it was all going to happen, but it did…

"I finally left the house in the late afternoon, with an invitation to call back for dinner that evening.

"Well, this went on for about a week. And then she suggested one evening that it was a pity I had to go home that night and wouldn't it be a good idea if I stayed overnight, using the guest bedroom.

" Fine,' I said. But the guest room turned out to be connected to her own by a small dressing room.

"Well, what the hell? What did I ever need the room for except to keep my clothes. It gradually became my room; I moved into the house lock, stock and barrel.

"Let me digress a little. I once heard two Texan oil men discussing English women. One's sole ambition was to sleep with a woman from the British aristocracy. She had to be genuine, with a line going back to

William the Conqueror. 'Hell, no,' said the other one. 'They'll be no good, just look at them, they're cold, tall, skinny, frigid, and undemonstrative.

"I smiled to myself and thought, ignorance is, in this case, no bliss.

"My Lady and I fell very much in love. Naked, she was astonishing. She had one of the finest and most beautiful bodies I have ever seen. And she was a fireball.

"With all humility, I confess one thing. She taught me a truth. Sex without intelligence is a bore.

"My Lady had the greatest physical attraction. Her body was firm and supple, she carried her breasts with a pride which I have seldom seen matched.

"Above all, she was completely unselfconscious. Her body was a sense of pride, her mind could match any man's.

"All right, she was wealthy, she was privileged, she was protected. But that wasn't all.

"I know too well from my own experiences just what the freedom she had inherited, freedom from poverty, freedom from want, freedom to say 'to hell with the world' can do to a personality; at one stage it nearly killed me — and I faced total moral ruin out of fantastic success.

"Yes, with the greatest affection I remember how much My Lady taught me. Later, I will tell you how much a girl from an orphanage taught me; nobility is nobility wherever you find it.

"I adored the Lady. I worshipped her. For her, wealth and a brilliant upbringing had meant simply the chance and opportunity to fulfil herself, intellectually, spiritually, physically, in fact, to expand her life to every limit.

"If she had been born a man, she would undoubtedly have been one of the nation's leaders. Even now she pulls enough weight.

"I adored her. Sex exploded into a fantasy of love; we couldn't leave each other alone. And each time it became more wonderful.

"It went wrong. On reflection, if I may coin a phrase, 'the difference in our stations' began to affect the relationship. The curious thing was that it affected me. It could not have mattered less to her. It did to me.

"In all honesty, money did not matter a twopenny damn to her. It is stupid, but I am sure that this only ever happens when you've been born with too much or when you've got nothing.

"The rot set in with a fancy dress suit. She had asked me to take her to a fancy dress ball and, thinking it would be fun, I said I would rake out some theatrical costumes for the occasion. But that wasn't what she wanted. She insisted that I be measured for an outfit and she wheeled in a tailor to take my measurements. I thought this a bit unnecessary, but I went along with it and sure enough, I got myself a dolly of an outfit. At least, it was a change from my corduroy suit which I normally wore for every occasion.

"It was about a week after the ball that she phoned me to say she had a nice surprise for me when I came home. She would not tell me what it was even when I arrived, but took me up to my bedroom. Well, that was no surprise to me, but then she said the real surprise was in the big, built-in wardrobe.

" 'What is it?' I said.

" 'Open the wardrobe and see.' Lady X smiled. 'I hope you don't mind, darling.

"When I opened the wardrobe, I was not so much surprised as stunned.

"There were six made-to-measure suits, half a dozen pairs of shoes, piles of hand-made shirts, new ties, socks and God knows what else. I was speechless.

"She followed that lot up with gold cufflinks, tie-pins, leather wallets, monogrammed silver-backed hairbrushes and a whole collection of expensive trinkets. Almost every evening, there was something, some little gift — it was like Christmas every day. In the end, I had to protest that I didn't need all this lavishness, but she said it pleased her to give me little presents — little presents? — so what could I do but accept it all?

"She told me she had more money than she could ever spend in her lifetime, and I certainly believed that. Most of her friends were in the 'Royal set'. At the time they were making just a little too many headlines in the newspapers and one had to be extremely discreet.

"I used to feel, at times, that they thought me a bit odd and found me amusing and something of a joke. Probably, I was wrong, but I couldn't help feeling it.

"With that crowd, I simply had to live on her money.

"If I had tried to stay independent I'd have been bankrupt inside a week because when we went out for an evening, it was always to the top places. I remember the first time this problem arose, when she told me we were taking two of her friends out to dinner at the Mirabelle or somewhere like that.

"At the time, I had about two quid in my pocket and I tactfully asked how the hell I was going to entertain four people on that kind of money.

" 'Don't worry, darling,' she said. 'I wouldn't dream of embarrassing you. If you wear your blue suit tonight, you'll find a new wallet in the coat with a few pounds in it.'

"And there was — except that the 'few pounds' was exactly one hundred and fifty pounds in fivers!

"Well, it sounds marvellous, but honestly, it used to make me feel terrible. Sure, she could afford it, but I began to think of myself as a leech, and it got harder and harder to live with.

"I don't think *she* ever thought about it. Simply, it would never occur to her. There was, in fact, a total lack of communication on one subject. She believed that all you had to do was to sit back and think about a problem and you could solve it. So you can with most things if you have enough money.

"Soon she began to tell me that I should not go on working in what she called 'that squalid little studio'. She wanted me to give up my theatrical work — which was coming along nicely — and to let her set me up with a plush studio in Mayfair where I could take society pictures more or less as a hobby.

"In vain did I try to explain that I liked my work, that it was satisfying to me and that I would not give up my own place, squalid or not. We began to quarrel about it and more than once I called it all off and walked out. But I loved her, so much, and I always went back — at least until it got so bad that I knew I simply had to stop it or I would be ruined as an individual.

"I just wanted to assert myself on what I considered to be equal terms. Now, of course, I realise just how unfair on her this attitude was.

"One day I decided that this would be it. I spent the night with her and the next morning I dressed in my favourite old green corduroy — which had been at the bottom of the wardrobe for months, out of her sight — took a last look round at the luxury which was still mine for the asking, and walked away from it.

"For a month, it drove me mad. She'd turn up at Gerrard Street in the Rolls and plead with me to come back, but I knew for sure that it wouldn't be any good to either of us. It was over, for good.

"I was pretty bloody miserable for a while, so I stuck grimly to the business of photography.

But Lucky Leo's always strike it rich. As I told you my good fortune turned up in the form of my dear of pal — Norman Wisdom."

CHAPTER 9

MARRIAGE AND PAM

MARRIAGE is of paramount importance to Harrison Marks. He is a difficult man for any woman to be married to by the simple nature of, if one may term it so, his calling.

His life is women, some of the most beautiful women in the world. From the first moment of his meeting with any one woman, his relationship with her must, necessarily be of a special nature.

The relationship is basically professional and yet can never be as analytical and detached as, say, that of a doctor.

Harrison Marks' task is to project his subjects in as an alluring, if necessary, as provocative and sexy a way as possible. He must, to a large extent, be involved with his subjects. Certainly, they must be sympathetic to him and he must like and understand them; emotionally there must be a close rapport.

"Let's face it," Harrison Marks explains. "We are attempting to portray emotion and it's not like photographing half-a-pound of chipolatas for an ad."

Any woman, no matter how superficially toughened, feels vulnerable in the raw: the very evidence of her sexuality, the fact that her nakedness is observed, and closely scrutinised, induces a degree of eroticism.

Many of the most experienced models are, quite simply, shy. They will not allow any visitors to a sitting, only the photographer and his assistant. With an audience, complete relaxation is impossible; they tense up, become self-conscious, even embarrassed: the session is ruined; essential intimacy between model and artist is destroyed.

But these are the daily conditions of work for Harrison Marks. Six hundred models through his hands a year.

A formidable challenge for any wife; a truly daunting obstacle for any marriage.

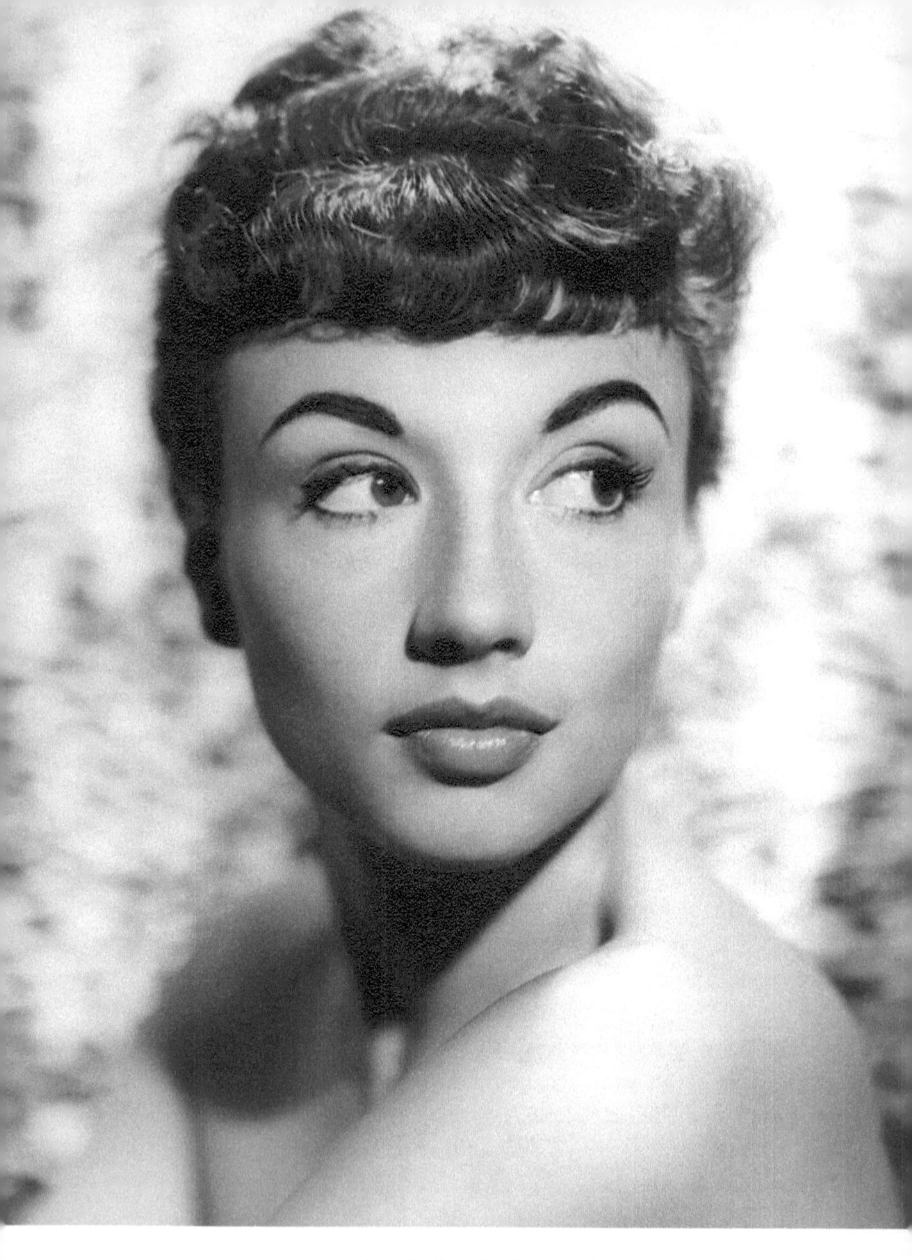

Pamela Green (1929 - 2010)

Yet for seven years of his second marriage, Harrison Marks was completely faithful. In common parlance one might say, he never looked at another woman.

Money, not sex, killed that marriage. Not a lack but a surfeit of it.

Too much of the stuff. Married bliss grew a little mouldy at the edges with a flood of green pound notes; love drowned in an ever deepening sea of crisp blue fivers.

It was a comfortable way to break-up, but it was a hell of a way to fail.

Harrison Marks is a committed womaniser. He is almost a compulsive marrier — from the age of 17 he has been at it. Marriage number one was born in boredom, "soul destroying" frustration and inexperience.

Harrison Marks was 17; his bride was 25.

It all started at the film laboratory during the days of "Chinese torture" — subtitling films.

From "I do" to decree absolute, it lasted altogether eight years. For four years they lived together.

It was hardly a harmonious relationship but Harrison Marks says: "I've nothing, absolutely nothing at all against her.

"If I tried my damnedest, I couldn't find anything bad to say against her.

On the contrary, she was a good sort. She stuck by me during the many troubles I found myself in at Brighton, and let's face it, no one puts up with poverty just for laughs.

"We just didn't hit it off. We rowed, we fought, we were disinterested in each other with nothing at all in common."

That, it seems, is the truth. , Eight years, and virtually not a memory to recall of the whole affair.

Unmemorable, a grey, nondescript period; a common-denominator existence punctuated only by disillusion, disagreements, the odd blazing rows and boredom.

Two incompatible people. Both to blame and neither responsible for the inevitable failure.

It ended, unremarkably, like a hundred thousand other similar marriages. How many other divorced husbands could really remember?

Then came Pam.

There is very little to forget about Pam. Few men in the Western world can have failed to see, and know, Pamela Green, almost intimately.

"She was, and still is, the greatest of them all," says Harrison Marks. Sooner or later she had to be called the pocket Venus. It was sooner.

Pamela Green is smallish but exquisitely, almost perfectly, formed.

Her face is classically modelled; high cheekbones, deep-set, large eyes, a perfect mouth. She is photographically excellent. On meeting her, one would not immediately say "what a beautiful woman," or even "what a striking woman".

But really beautiful women, in the accepted, conventional sense of the word, rarely do photograph well.

It takes time to appreciate Pam. She is, in a crowded room, attractive, good-looking and a presence.

In front of the camera she is supreme and a very rare beauty.

The fact is that almost every barrack-room, mess-deck and workshop, a multitude of offices, clubs and men's restrooms everywhere have, at one time or another, pinned up Pamela Green. Next to the Venus de Milo, hers is probably the best-known body the world has ever seen.

Her breasts are firm, strong and large; the torso is superbly muscled, slim, active and supple; her legs excellent and shapely.

Altogether, she is splendidly a woman — a whole woman.

It is a salutary thought that Pamela Green has introduced more emergent youths to sex than any other woman in history.

She could be called, quite accurately, the fourth form primer to nakedness.

How many teenage boys have ever seen a naked woman until they look at pictures of Pamela?

In private life, she is a naturally charming woman; a modest and moral woman of considerable talent. Her paintings have been hung at the Royal Academy; she still paints. She is also an accomplished classical pianist.

Her attributes are loyalty and love; she has loved very deeply — probably still does.

About the marriage:

It all began through Bernard Delfont who took Harrison Marks on as a theatrical photographer.

Pam was one of the Follies girls at the Prince of Wales Theatre, London.

Which in itself, is curious. Her background doesn't fit into the show-girl image. Anglo-Dutch by birth, her mother comes from Holland. As a child, she lived in a prosperous home at West Wickham in Kent.

Captain Green, Pam's father, had a distinguished Naval career. Before the war he was with the Ellerman Bucknell line, he had been at sea since he was 16 and was thinking of giving it up.

But the war changed all that: he transferred from the Merchant Navy to the Royal Navy and his fighting days started. He was sunk in the *Orford* which, as he says, rather upset him. Then came the really rough times on Russian convoys. Eventually, he was an acting Captain, commanding the *Switha* on anti-submarine work in the Faroes. A versatile family this; in his spare time and at night school he studied architecture he qualified and now practises in London.

Pam's mother's family were all surgeons in Holland; there were five or six doctors in the family.

Her first schooling was at a local school in The Hague. She left on the last plane out of Holland before the German occupation. After that the family followed father around and Pam went to some 14 schools before she settled, for the longest period, at St. Martin's School of Art. She won a grant for the Royal Academy School.

"It was so small, it really wasn't worth having," she explains, "so I went into the theatre, in the Follies Bergere."

In reality, quite a break from the professional background of her home life.

Perhaps it was as well that Father gave up the sea when he did. A couple of years later you would have had the situation of the captain on the bridge in all his brass-buttoned and gold-braided glory and down below his daughter displayed on all the sailors' lockers — without a button or a braid to her name. Not, perhaps, good for Naval discipline, but splendid for morale

Her early days were spent equally between her British home and at the estate of her Mother's family in Wassenaar near The Hague, Holland. Consequently, she is completely bi-lingual, speaking Dutch as perfectly as she does English.

Then came the Prince of Wales Theatre and George Harrison Marks.

Now this was in the days of early pin-up photography, all sequins, spangles and ostrich feathers. It was part of Harrison Marks' job to photograph her.

"From the word go," Harrison Marks says, "a tremendous thing sparked; it was a very big affair." It must have been. A Follies girl is not usually without friends and seldom without offers — perhaps it would be more accurate to describe them as propositions. Life is right at the centre of the glitter belt. And it can be sweet and rewarding.

But the young Harrison Marks had little to offer. To be precise, he had the studio in Gerrard Street and a sideboard.

When the studio closed, the doors of the sideboard opened and a single bed unfolded. That was it, no carpet, no easy chairs; just studio props and a folding bed.

Apart from that he was in debt and being pressed. For the first time in his life he had commitments like rent, telephone, rates, electricity, and the essentials for running a studio.

Often, when the money did come in, it was a toss-up between paying the bills or a binge. "Usually, the binge won,' he says.

In spite of all, Pam moved in. And that was the beginning of life with a sex symbol who was to become virtually a sex goddess.

Harrison Marks says simply "Pam set me up; she started it all — in many ways I owe much to her."

They were very much in love. So life in Gerrard Street settled into its routine. What was to prove a comparatively comfortable routine for a few weeks at least, but hardly in comfortable surroundings.

A rotary glazer for the photographic business was out of the question. So when the day's work was done and the prints had been developed and washed, two fishermen's nets used as studio props, were slung across the room. The prints, sometimes hundreds of them, were laid carefully on them to dry and the loving couple crawled underneath to sleep in their sideboard love-nest.

Came the day when Harrison Marks had been away all afternoon photographing a commission.

He arrived home tired to Pam, who said, with an air of utter resignation and no recriminations: "They've taken the bed away; a man from the h.p. (hire purchase) company came."

"It only cost about sixteen quid," Harrison Marks explains. "And the repayments weren't more than 6s. 2d. a week. Still, they reclaimed it."

Bediess, they retired for the night. Down came the studio drapes to be folded into a makeshift mattress. "Surprisingly comfortable it was," says Harrison Marks on reflection. That is how they lived for months.

Things had been tough and were getting tougher.

Not that Harrison Marks was not making money. He was, by nature, a Bohemian, and the studio became a centre for Bohemians and layabouts in Soho. What he earned, he boozed away. In that free-and-easy Soho Bohemian atmosphere, a lot of money went on spongers; one of these played almost as important a part as Pam in setting up the success that was to come later.

The Major, a well known Soho "con man", had attached himself to the studio, ostensibly as Harrison Marks' agent. "Altogether," he says, "the Major knocked me for about £300 on all sorts of things. For instance, he ran up one telephone bill of £38."

Things had indeed been catching up. "I was in real sticky trouble," says Harrison Marks. "I owed about £260."

In desperation, he had approached Harry Kweller, the small printer who had done his first 50 visiting cards and later his letterheads and brochures and borrowed £250.

That lasted no time at all. The agreement was that it should be paid back in small weekly instalments. Harry Kweller was not a rich man, and Harrison Marks had failed to keep up his repayments.

"He was a nice, sweet man," Harrison Marks explains. "But he had only a tiny printing shop and he couldn't afford to lose 250.

"So he cut up shirty and demanded his cash back. "I don't blame him at all, but I hadn't even got 250 pennies, let alone 250 quid.

"Anyway, he came round to the studio one night with his accountant, Harry Ruben, and he started to cut up really rough.

"He threatened to close me down and sell me up, though what there was to sell wouldn't have brought more than a few bob.

"I honestly couldn't blame him, he was very upset; I felt really terrible."

It was, in its way, a classic situation: the angry creditor with his accountant advisor and the penniless debtor who just wanted to be shot of the pair of them. And would promise anything just as long as they would GO.

Ruben tried to calm down Kweller and to arrive at some compromise solution — without, it must be admitted, very much hope.

Suddenly the situation was transformed. Out of the blue Pam said: "I'll let you have half the money, Mr. Kweller, £125, and we'll try to start the repayments again and keep them up."

There was silence… from all parties.

She went on: "I'll get the money from the bank tomorrow and bring it round to your office."

Of course, everyone agreed. Ruben, however, laid down one condition, Marks himself must bring the cash to his, Ruben's, office in the morning. Harrison Marks said yes. "I would have agreed to anything they suggested," he explains. "All I wanted was to see the back of them; I wanted them out of the studio."

That was surprise number one. Surprise number two came immediately and it was even more curious.

Ruben turned to Kweller and said: "Look, Harry, it's the best way. I'll take the responsibility for the other half of the cash myself."

The creditors left and then in a fit of self-criticism, or more probably, self-pity, Harrison Marks turned to Pam, "Where are you going to get the cash?" he demanded.

She replied: "I've got £150 in the bank; we'll use that."

"What on earth do you want to do that for? Don't be a fool, keep it there." The self-recrimination flowed thick and fast.

"Look, why waste it on a bum like me? Why waste your time with me? Why don't you get out?

"I'm no good. I'm irresponsible — it will never work out." So on and so on.

All Pam said very quietly was: "You're the best photographer I've ever seen. You've got it in your hands to be the best in the world."

She paused and added: ". . . and I'm going to see you are."

The meeting the following day was to prove the most decisive in the Harrison Marks career.

Significantly, this incident showed the inner depths behind that facade of superb gland and flesh. Pam Green was to prove a power.

They were in love and like most lovers their path was not roses, roses all the way. But in this case, it could have been harder from a different direction; Pam's family who, some might consider, curiously, did everything they could to help.

Pam's background was respectable, suburban, almost staid. Her parents, Harrison says, are among the kindest, sweetest, people he has ever met.

"Think of it," he says. "It must have been a terrible shock to them to have this drunken, layabout bum; this broke Bohemian in a green corduroy suit dropped into their family circle.

"Never once did they complain, never did they offer a word of reproach or criticism.

"Their view was — if this is the man Pam loves, we'll do our best to make it work."

They always did. Even when the thing broke up there were no recriminations and today, everyone in this quadrangle is on good terms with everyone else, and they are all genuinely fond of each other.

At the Kweller Ruben meeting in the studio and after Pam's loyalty and trust had stopped Harrison Marks in his tracks, he confesses "She saw something in me I couldn't see. I just could not visualise myself as a top photographer; I hadn't the self-confidence to think of myself in the world class.

"She could; it baffled me."

Came the morning and the visit to Ruben's office. Ruben opened up: "As a client," he said, "you're absolutely useless to me and I'm an idiot even to bother with you.

"Let's forget what happened last night, because I can tell you that for six months Harry Kweller has been telling me about you — he's never stopped saying how bloody clever you are… as a photographer.

"Well, I looked at the pictures on your walls last night, and I've never seen photographs like those ever before."

Ruben went on: "I think it's a crime to let someone like you sink — so I'll handle your affairs. But you've of to come and see me every week without fail.

That started it and since then Ruben and Harrison Marks have met every Monday morning "without fail".

Harrison Marks' testimonial is uncomplicated: "The best friend I ever had."

To this day, without Ruben, Harrison Marks will not lift one finger. "He's guided me through ups acid downs, been responsible for keeping me out of trouble and we have developed a complete mutual trust.

"Now he's my partner in the film business. I put a plan to him which will cost £50,000 and I don't even have to explain it.

"All he says is, 'Right George, if you feel it's the right thing to do, here's my 25,000!

"And this is very, very curious because we are such totally different characters.

"We live utterly different lives — absolutely separate lives. He is a quiet, home-loving man who adores his wife. He has two grown-up boys.

"Half, more than half, the things I do must make his hair stand on end."

But on that morning in 1952 Harrison Marks and Pam went back to work with about 1s. 4d. in their pockets, hope and a new confidence in their hearts.

Harrison Marks first got the idea of pin-up pictures when he was photographing Pam as a Follies girl.

He thought: "People always crowd round to look at them; there must be a market for them."

There was. Magazines bought them and this led to stage two.

A magazine editor had been round to the studio looking at prints and transparencies. As he was leaving, he said: "Oh, by-the-way, George, we're putting one of your pictures and your name on the cover next issue, it will be a big puller for us and it's an honour for you."

Harrison Marks thought: "Great." Then he had second thoughts: "If it could be as big a puller as that and worth it to them to put it on the front, why not publish his own magazine?"

All the material was there, but to launch a magazine costs rather more than 1s. 4d., which was the extent of the studio's uncommitted capital. They needed backing for 3,500.

Well, optimism is free and enthusiasm runs out only when the legs are too tired to carry it any further. The idea seemed good to them, even great. So off they went knocking on printers' and publishers' doors. The replies were illuminating, ranging from: "Get out"; "Drop dead"; "How

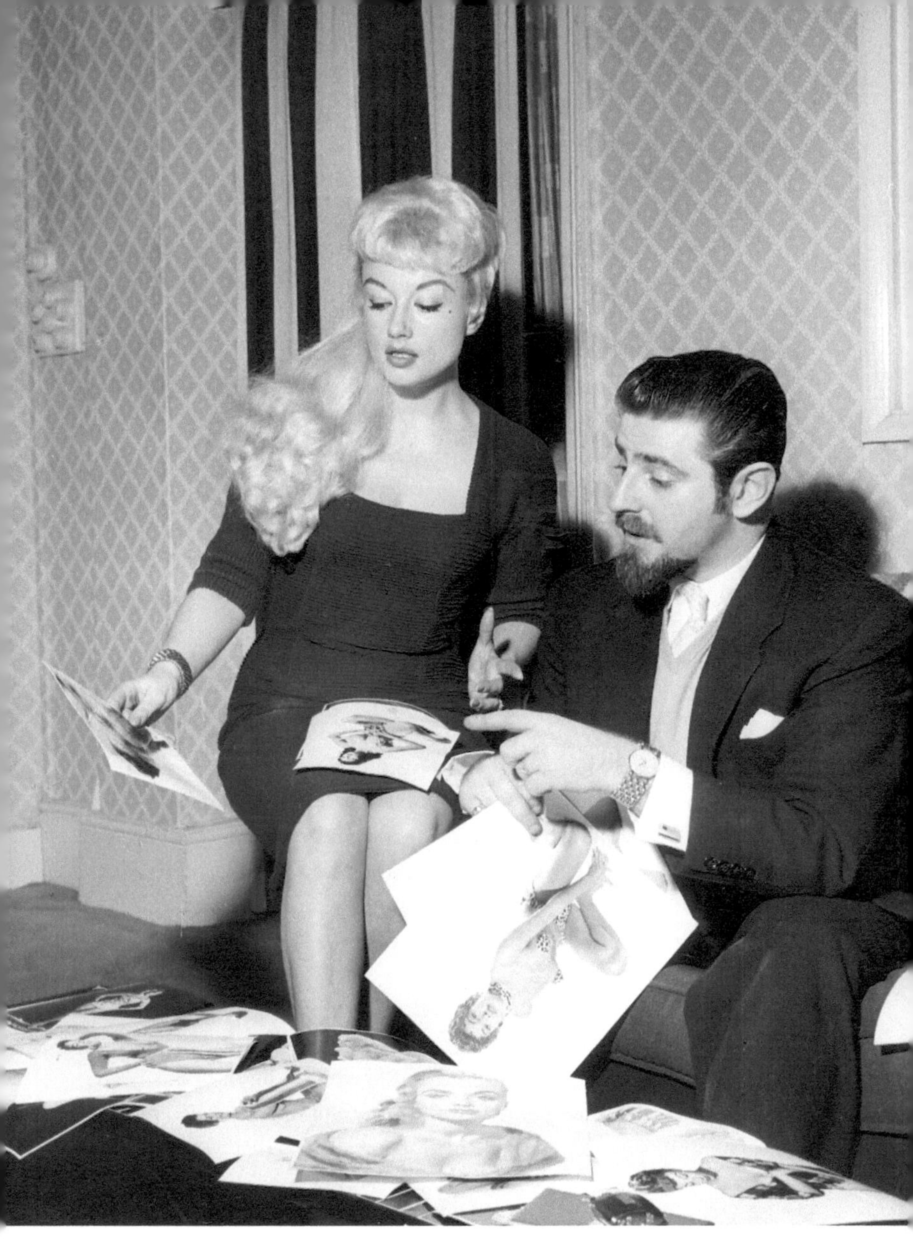

Pamela Green and George Harrison Marks choosing images at the Gerrard Street studio

dare you bring me pictures like that"; "I'll call the police"; "Do you think I'm a fool?"; "3,500 to publish rubbish — you must be mad"; "You're a confidence trickster"; "I would be arrested".

Minds were very, very narrow in those days and nobody would even consider printing a book of nudes. The idea, it seemed, had run out of steam in a hiss of chatter and pleading, and the bitter disillusion of flogging a seemingly dead horse.

Despondently Pam and Harrison Marks sat in the studio licking their wounds. Immobilised, it seemed, as if by their own fixative.

Re-enter the Major, the "con" man who had nothing at all left in the world but optimism; his sole trading asset — good hope, a glib tongue and an unfailing eye for a fast buck.

Unfortunately for the poor fellow the speed of the hand always defeated the eye, and the "fast bucks" slipped through his fingers far more quickly than he was able to spot them.

On this occasion, he did know a printer who wasn't in a much better position than Harrison Marks.

But he had a shop, three assistants, a clapped-out flat-bed press and he could raise £3,500 on credit from his suppliers.

Harrison Marks met Jim Martin, jobbing printer, also of Soho.

Clearly, in Mr. Martin's mind, there were reservations. He was the man who, if he wasn't exactly putting up the hard cash, was mortgaging his credit and livelihood. Still, after great deliberation, he said yes.

They agreed to publish a 24-page magazine call it *Kamera* and print 15,000 copies to sell at half-a-crown. The blocks were made, the paper was ordered. They were in it far too deep to pull out, so they crossed their fingers and wished for luck.

Luck came. Bonanza. The beginning of the goldrush; the giddy headiness of success, the ecstasy of riches; the despair of well-breeched misery; the corruption of wealth; the sweetness of power — all that was to happen started when Mr. Martin said:

"I'll stake you."... It happened for both of them.

And it took years, two great traumatic experiences in love and a searchingly bitter involvement before Harrison Marks got his feet back on the ground.

In two days, *Kamera* sold out — all 15,000 copies. The orders poured in. It was reprint, reprint, reprint until the arms all but fell off the old printing press.

For five weeks the rush went on unabated. The only thing that stopped it was a second issue.

More than 150,000 copies of *Kamera* No. 1 were sold, grossing £18,750. Harrison Marks' share was 1s. a copy — £7,500. And the money was rolling in at the same rate every month.

At last, the man who eight weeks previously found it hard to raise 250 pennies, could afford to buy Pam a bed. The days were hectic, the nights were… comfortable.

Success had started on tick, but it was an end forever to happiness on the never-never. Now it was joy for cash, crinkly, crisp green, blue, brown bank notes by the barrow load.

Harrison Marks had arrived and ironically it was ladies with nothing — nothing on at all, that is, who had put him there.

CHAPTER 8

Life in Soho

SUDDENLY, unexpectedly, life was good in the Gerrard Street household. Money was cascading in, the sweet smell of success — a current phrase at the time — permeated the studio flat and happiness seemed assured. But, in Soho, life is seldom quite what it seems on the surface.

In the beginning, we noted that life was not just a bunch of pretty faces for Harrison Marks. To Pam's despair and his horror, here, on his doorstep, in fact under his very room in the basement club below the studio, there appeared the frightening, ugly faces of brutality. Dramatic it may sound, but it is no exaggeration to say that by night terror stalked the streets outside.

"I swear," says Harrison Marks, "that I have seen corpses lying in the gutter in that street. Dead bodies which were whipped away in the nick of time before the police arrived."

In 1952, Gerrard Street was the "front line" for one of the most vicious outbreaks of gang warfare which London has ever known.

Who was who, what was what and why they were battling could never be discovered. In truth, members of the studio were too terrified to ask.

The club had changed hands. Previously it had been run by two sweet old dears, former theatricals, but now it had become the headquarters and drinking haunt of one of the mobs. Harrison Marks says: "They were some of the ugliest customers I have ever seen outside Grand Guignol, and I can tell you there were some really rough villains knocking about in those days."

The gang under the studio were apparently sworn enemies of other gangs which gathered in two other clubs down the street.

Almost nightly, razor and bottle fights broke out. Not just a couple of thugs fighting it out, but whole gangs of villains laying about each other with broken bottles, cut-throat razors, sharpened bicycle chains, stilettos, flick knives, knuckledusters — the whole armoury of brutal thuggery. There were savage outbreaks of fighting, the pavements and gutters would run with blood.

"I don't mind admitting it, when the police asked questions, I knew nothing," Harrison Marks confesses. "I was really terrified, and I knew that if I upset these villains, it would be all up with me long, long before the police could come to my help. And the thugs were determined to let me know, in unmistakable terms, just how vulnerable my position was.

"After one particularly bad blood-letting, a deputation came to see me. Two characters came into the studio and asked if I had seen anything.

" ' No,' I said. 'Not a thing.'

" 'Sure?' they said. 'You wouldn't, like, talk to the rozzers about it?'

" 'Definitely not,' I said. 'How could I, I just told you, I didn't see anything.'

"They smiled, if you could call it a smile: 'Good. Because if you was to… And one of them ran a finger across his throat; a gesture which got the message across in the sort of visual terms I appreciated. And, believe me, you wouldn't blame me for staying dumb if you had seen it.

"A number of men died during that outbreak. Eventually, there were gunnings in broad daylight, which really shocked the public conscience.

"It got so bad that I put in two extra doors on the stairs leading up to my place, AND had steel reinforcement put on the front door of the studio for more than once the gangs smashed down the first two, thinking my place was a hideaway for some members of the opposition gangs. I don't mind admitting I was scared, and Pam was terrified. When we went out to a movie or something at night, we'd spend a couple of hours afterwards in a coffee shop, arriving home at the studio in the early hours of the morning, rather than walk down Gerrard Street late at night in case there was a sudden punch-up.

"We learned to live with it. After all, there was nothing else we could do."

The seamy underworld bubbled in Soho, as one can safely presume, it always will. Few of the fun-seeking crowds which thronged the area night after night were remotely aware of what was going on. Fun and entertainment were what they were seeking, and there was plenty to be found.

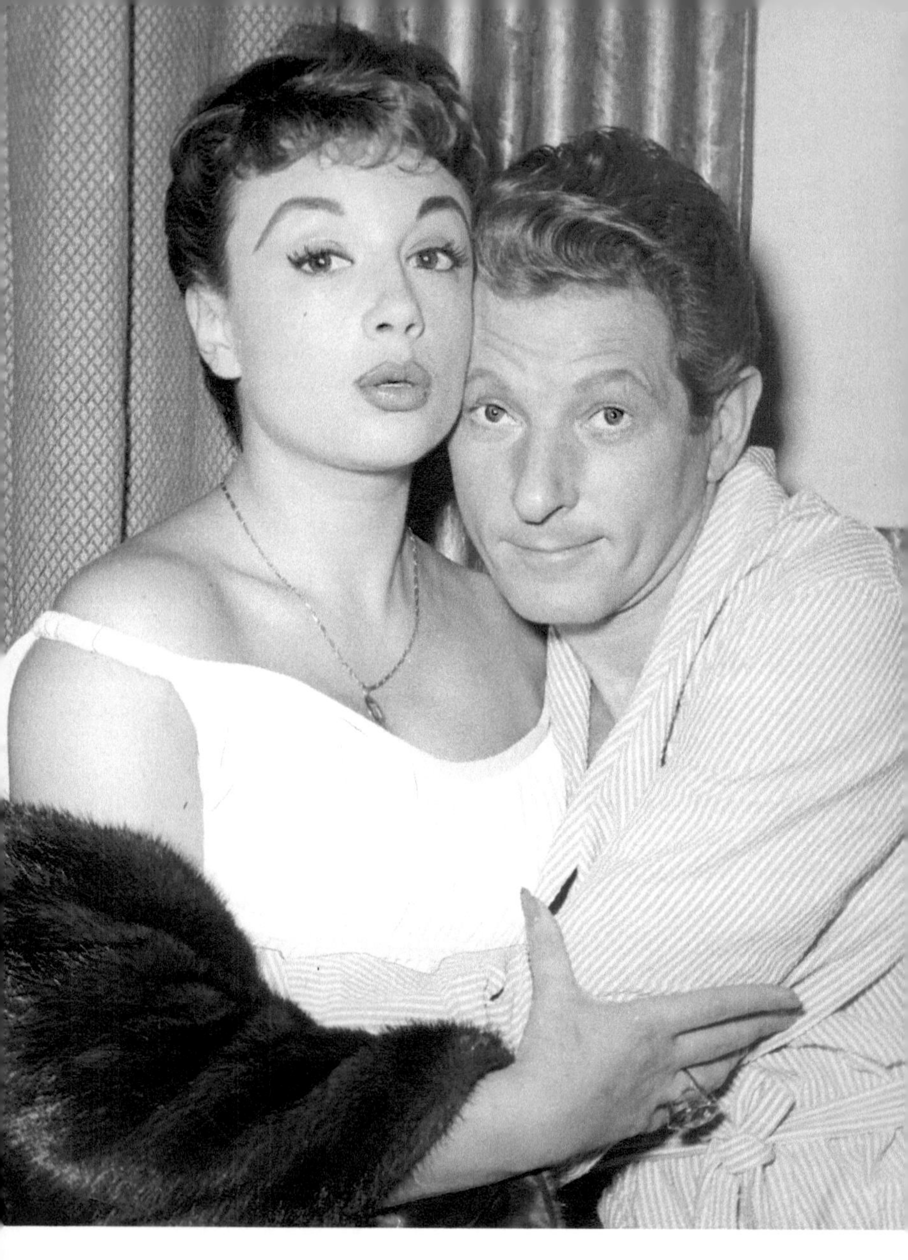

Pamela Green and Danny Kaye, the American actor

Theatre posters announced personal appearances of the big names in show-business. Top of all the world's variety theatres, the Palladium, pulled the greatest international stars. To top the bill here put the ultimate seal of success on any artist's career.

They all came: Jack Benny, Nat King Cole, Danny Kaye, Guy Mitchell, Jimmy Durante, and many, many more.

Until *Kamera* was a smash hit, theatrical photographs were Harrison Marks' main business. He photographed them all.

Only one out of the torrent of talent ever, at the Palladium, gave him a rough ride.

That was Danny Kaye. Kaye is an enigma. He works unpaid until he is nearly dropping from exhaustion for the United Nations Children's Fund. He is passionately, earnestly devoted to the cause, and not in any way to seek publicity from it. Much of his hardest work is done quietly, quite unheralded and with great sincerity; rather than seek acclaim, Kaye uses the pulling power of his name to keep the fund rolling. A dedicated, sincere and clearly a good man.

Yet few celebrities have excelled his aptitude for antagonising people and losing friends — particularly the Press.

Fifteen years ago, he disliked the Press — and even now, there is little love lost between them. For a man with such a genius for instant communication and sympathy, which he certainly commands on stage, this almost total block, this barrier between him and the other mass communicators is, to say the least, curious.

It was Kaye's second season over here at the time when Harrison Marks met him, and he was still smarting from the beating he had taken from British newspapers. He had made some remark about Royalty which had not gone down too well, and the papers had really burned him up.

Harrison Marks remembers the situation well, perhaps a little too well: "When he came over, this time, he refused absolutely to meet the Press, except on one occasion when he called a Press conference to talk about his work for UNICEF — the United Nations Children's Fund. Dozens of reporters turned up at the Palladium to talk to him in his dressing room, but he allowed only one photographer — me.

"The Press conference got off to a bad start because a reporter asked a question about Kaye's private life and that brought a venomous reply that set the tone for the whole thing. Furthermore, when I flashed off my first picture, I caught Danny in mid-sentence, and he just stopped and turned a look on me which would have frozen an Eskimo.

"I suppose it was the tension coupled with that withering glance which unsettled me, but I remember I felt most unhappy throughout the session, and I was damned glad when it was all over. I dashed outside to hand the film to my darkroom man who was going to rush back to the studio and work through the night developing and printing the pictures since I had arranged with a number of papers and magazines to give them the prints the following day. And when I had handed the stuff over, I went for a drink. I met another photographer, and we stood there talking for maybe half-an-hour before I headed back to the studio.

"But when I got there — calamity! There was my darkroom man with his head in his hands, looking like death. He didn't say a word when I walked in, but just pointed to a strip of film hanging up to dry and my heart hit my boots with a thud.

" 'No good?' I asked, knowing damned well what the answer was going to be.

" 'No good,' he said.

"When I looked at the strip of film, I understood his depression. I had just one picture on it — the first one I had banged off. The rest were just transparent celluloid. I knew instinctively what it was and barely had to look at the camera to confirm it. In my flustered state after that chilling look from Danny Kaye, I had re-set the camera on the wrong synchronisation, which meant that the flash went off before the lens shutter opened, and, of course, I got nothing on the film.

" 'Oh, Christ!' I groaned. 'What am I going to do?' No one in the studio had any good answers, but it was quite obvious that, somehow or other, I would have to get in to see Danny Kaye again and ask him to let me have a few more shots. And I knew that it wasn't going to be easy.

"The next morning, I rushed round to the Dorchester, where Kaye's party was staying, and collared his manager. I told him a tale that would have brought tears from a stone, and he was very sympathetic but doubted whether he could get me in to see Danny again. I pleaded with him to try, telling him I would lose my job if I didn't get the pictures and that would mean the kids would starve, and I'd go to jail — anything

I could think of to put my case across. In the end, he told me to go to the Palladium that night and wait outside Danny Kaye's dressing room, and he would see what he could do.

"More in hope than expectation, I turned up at 6.15. I waited like a lemon in the corridor outside the star dressing room until 10.30 when at last, Kaye's manager came out and spoke to me.

"All right,' he said. 'Danny will give you a few minutes.'

"Kaye was sitting sprawled in an armchair, and he gave me a look of utter contempt.

"I was going to make some apology for disturbing him again and throw in some crack about what a berk I was — but he beat me to it. 'You sure must be a stinking lousy photographer,' was his opening remark, and when I went to say something in reply, he again cut me short. 'OK, OK, get on with it. I'll give you three minutes.' There wasn't time to do anything but swallow my pride and get on with the job. I took about five shots of him sitting, and then he suddenly stood up: That's it,' he snapped curtly and walked out.

"Well, maybe I was a bloody nuisance. But in my book, that's still a pretty crummy way to treat anyone."

The bitterness still rankles, and it is tinged with sadness that such a great artist could behave in that way.

Harrison Marks says: "What a contrast to the other big names I photographed in those wonderful Palladium days. Jack Benny, who always ordered tea with all the trimmings for anyone who went to see him backstage; Guy Mitchell, whose dressing room literally ran with booze in a continual swinging party where everyone was welcome; Laurel and Hardy, full of olde worlde charm and grace; and dear old Jimmy Durante.

"I remember Jimmy gave me about three solid hours of his time to take all the pictures I wanted — and then ordered three hundred prints from me as hand-outs to autograph. I'm sure he didn't really need that many and I suspect he was doing me a favour. A really great guy."

Soho was gay and garish. The Wolfenden Act had hardly been thought of, and the streets were packed with prostitutes. They jostled each other on the crowded pavements.

These were the Harrison Marks's neighbours, their flats, adjoined the studio. Almost every building housed at least one "brass" often many more.

Once the visitors clear out, Soho quickly becomes a village again with its own entity and communal life. Neighbours here are like neighbours anywhere, either you like or loathe them, no matter what their calling.

The Harrison Marks family grew fond of their community. "You know, some of them were really sweet and wonderful people, you forgot what they were and what they did and came to like them for themselves. Just because a woman takes up the oldest profession, it doesn't necessarily mean that she ceases to be a human being.

"They were kind to us. But I used to hold the most bizarre conversations and be really genuinely interested. One grew so used to it that it didn't seem at all odd. It could have been a Dagenham housewife telling her neighbour how her old man was working at Fords: ' 'e done 15 hours overtime this week, luv, made about nine quid extra.' Only *my* chats with *my* neighbours went like this, often as not:

" 'Hello, Georgie, lovie. I've had a wonderful day, darling. I've seen 30 clients already… marvellous, isn't it? Getting a bit tired now, though. Think I'll pack it up for the day… you be in the pub later? I'll see you then.'

"And, honestly, I wouldn't bat an eyelid and often as not, without really thinking, I'd reply: 'Isn't that wonderful, I'm so pleased for you.' "

One by one they came to know them all. There was Daphne with the educated voice.

Daphne worked only from Monday to Friday. She always dressed in tweeds, very expensive tweeds and at the weekend she went to her "house' in the country.

It wasn't a house at all, to be truthful; it was a very fine hotel, an old inn. And she owned it, virginia creeper, converted coach houses, fine old courtyard and all.

The staff would say to inquiries during the week: "Madam runs a business in Town during the week; this place is really her hobby." They hadn't the faintest idea.

Round the bar, the county set would comment: Brilliant woman, got her head screwed on the right way — got a man's brain."

She was extremely highly regarded and respected. And she was wealthy.

One character came to dominate Gerrard Street: the Harrison Marks old tabby tom cat, Uncle. Uncle died in 1965, aged 21. Everybody knew him; there wasn't a single restaurant in the area from which he hadn't been slung out. He plagued the life out of Mario, who ran the Italian restaurant opposite the studio. He was always in there. A customer would be sitting eating his meal when, like a flash of lightning, a paw would shoot out, and a steak would disappear.

Mario was excitable; he would scream: "Datta blooty cat . .. I murder heem," and, whoosh! Uncle was through the door to safety. But he had an uncanny second sense; he knew exactly which of the pair of legs which stopped to read the menu, would actually go inside. He clung to them and back he would slink.

Then the almighty row would break out again, Mario would scream, and Pam would become embarrassed.

"For Christ's sake, pretend we don't know him," Harrison Marks would hiss, ignoring Uncle.

Uncle respected their judgment; he never ever approached them in a restaurant.

The day came when Uncle took a mistress — a human one.

Michelle was a famous French "brass". Big, fat and blousy, with one-inch eyelashes and lurid make-up. Though she had lived here for years, she had never lost her accent. She was a great gal, with a passionate love for animals. She took to Uncle immediately, and he responded.

At 9 o'clock every morning Uncle slid out of the studio for his assignation with Michelle. Michelle's maid would buy ½lb. of best calve's liver for him. His day was set.

Michelle seldom talked of anything else but Uncle. "Your Uncle," she would tell the Harrison Marks', "is a very educated cat… he sits at the bottom of my bed all day and watches."

The drawback to the relationship was that Michelle could never resist talking about Uncle; she would ramble on for never less than 20 minutes every time she met Harrison Marks.

Going to lunch one day, Pam and George spotted Michelle on her pitch at the corner of the street. "Cross over," said Harrison Marks, "I'm too rushed to waste half-an-hour with her today."

At lunch-time Gerrard Street is crowded with a milling throng. Nevertheless, Michelle spotted them. For some curious reason, whenever she saw the Harrison Marks' she assumed they were looking for Uncle. This day was no exception. Right across the street above the noise of the traffic she screamed at the top of her powerful voice: "Eef you are looking for your Uncle, Georgie, hee's oopstairs in my flat lying on the bed. 'Ees worn out, poor old dear." The street stopped!

A Cockney woman bystander said: "I'n'it a shame, poor old sod; they ought to look after him proper."

A bowler-hatted passing man simply exclaimed: "Disgusting! "

Far less wholesome characters abounded in those seedy streets, too. No matter how tough they are, the evilest villains are not villainous all the time; only most of the time and they can develop friendships, requiring nothing in return.

One such rogue took a liking to George. He is still around the area, so his name had better be left out. At the time, he was working as a chuckerout for one of the clubs. He was known for his aptitude for slashing people; two chivs in his pocket were his stock in trade and he was really a very tough customer.

"I've seen some of the people he had cut up," Harrison Marks explains. "He really mutilated them, in a matter of seconds.

"Every so often, he would disappear for a time. He was proud of the fact that he had done some 20 years in gaol.

"He showed me his back one day: I was shattered. It was a mass of scars. I think he must have been one of the last people to get the 'cat'.

"For some reason, he took a great liking to me. He would wander up and say, 'Hello, Mr. George; everything all right? Anyone getting in your hair? Anyone you'd like fixing? Just say the word, you know; anything to oblige you.' It put me in a fix one day when I met Stuart Samuels in a pub for a quiet drink. Every time we met we kidded each other along — we always did it. Suddenly, in walked my 'slasher' friend and the usual conversation took place… anyone getting in your hair? And all the rest of it.

"Stuart and I were having a joke together, and my friend stood by, 'Sure there's no one you need fixing?' he asked again. We were still joking and off the cuff I said, 'Come to think of it, this berk's getting on my wick a bit,' and I pointed to Stuart. The effect was paralysing. The great hands shot out, grabbed Stuart by the lapels and lifted him off his feet. 'For God's sake,' I screamed. 'I'm only kidding.' I had to bellow at him — kidding, kidding, having a joke; he's a great pal of mine… Like you, I added hurriedly, 'For Pete's sake, put him down.' There was cold sweat round my collar. 'Kidding,' he asked. 'Sure,' I said. 'I thought you liked a joke.' " 'You quite sure you're kidding?' he asked again. " 'Positive.'

" 'A joke, yes — I like a joke. Well, if you're sure you're only kidding, Mr. George, I'll nip off.'

"If that had happened outside I dread to think what would have happened to dear old Stuart. My blood runs cold; I had seen some of my 'friend's victims."

This man lived for violence. It was his sole mode of life. Harrison Marks believes that he had some deep psychological disturbance. Undoubtedly he had a slight touch of madness. Seemingly no one during his 20 years confinement had attempted to diagnose it. There were even more frightening elements: they came up during another casual meeting. The conversation had gone exactly to the previous pattern until there came this macabre twist. Harrison Marks relates: "I'd thanked him very much for the offer, as usual, and declined his services. Then he suddenly sprang this one. 'Is there anyone you'd like to be rid of?' he asked. 'You know, someone you'd like to get lost… permanently?'

" 'It can be arranged, you know. Dead easy. Just you mention it, if you think of anyone… it'll only cost 50 quid.'

"The horrible thing is that he wasn't joking."

When Harrison Marks was in Brighton he had taken a set of very good pictures of Norman Wisdom at the time he was just perfecting his "little man" bit, when Bernard Delfont picked him to star in the Follies show at the Prince of Wales and really launched the little man in a big way.

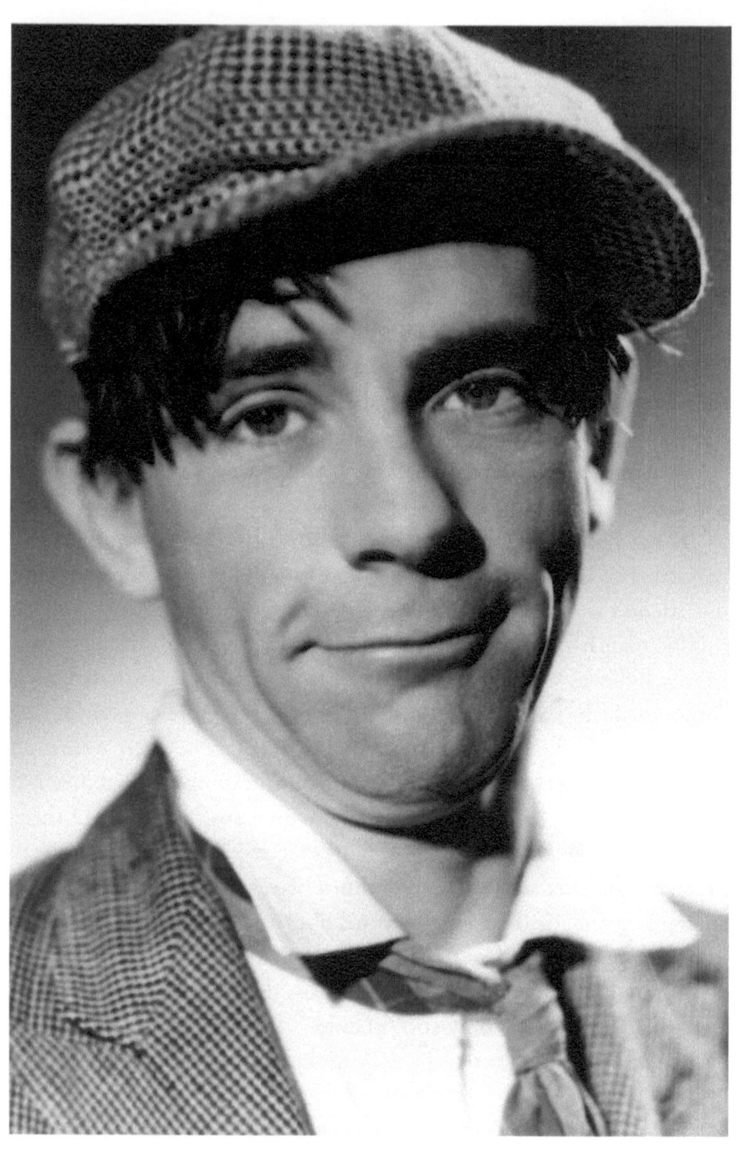

Norman Wisdom (1915-2010), English actor and comedian

Norman produced the pictures. Delfont was impressed enough to offer a job as a cameraman for the new show — a job which literally put Harrison Marks among the stars.

Even so, it was by no means roses, roses all the way. By diligence and application to the old boy's mail-order business, Harrison Marks had been able to make enough to move from the brothel to a first-floor studio flat in Gerrard Street. Now there was a stiff rent to pay, rates and the rest. Providence, alas, was not one of this adventurer's stronger virtues.

"Big deal?" he says. "Nothing like it. I was still hard up, still struggling along with the odd job or two, but now, apart from the rent to pay, I had a lot of equipment on the old never-never, and it was usually a struggle to find the instalments. That was Harrison Marks a decade ago

"Working for myself, I had picked up a few theatrical jobs but the folding stuff was still pretty hard to come by and I depended a lot on casual studio sittings, portraits of actors, and so on. As a matter of fact, my first customer in Gerrard Street was a struggling rep. actor named Kenneth Hughes — and Ken Hughes is now one of the world's top film directors.

"But once, when I was in a pretty desperate state, I was given a considerable shot in the wallet by a bloke I can only describe as the most bizarre character I have ever met. He literally burst into the office. Six feet six and about as broad, he thundered through the door and boomed: "My name is Paddy Orford Smith. You will now take my picture.'

"Just like that.

"Naturally, I was delighted. I made an appointment for him for the next day and looked forward to a few guineas in the coffers.

"The following day, he turned up with a suitcase full of clothes, saying he wanted pictures in a variety of costumes and poses. Now, normally, I took 20 shots on a plate camera for a job like this, but I must admit that this fellow completely overpowered me, insisting on being taken from every angle and in every corny old theatrical pose you ever saw. In the end, I had worked through well over a hundred plates 1 And when he was done, he swept out, telling me to contact him with the proofs at his London hotel.

"A few days later, when I'd ground out all the proofs, I staggered out with them and headed for the hotel. I was dead worried, I must admit, because I had decided that unless he paid for all the cost of the materials I had used, I'd be well out of pocket since the most you could expect an unknown actor to order was half a dozen ten-by-eight prints and a dozen postcards.

"But when I showed them all to Orford Smith, I nearly fell over. 'I'll have one of each,' he roared. The biggest prints you can make.' I started to mutter something about the cost and then this fellow dived into his pocket and pulled out a hand-roll like a sailor's hammock — all fivers. He peeled off a wedge of them and handed them over and ushered me out of the room with orders to bring back the pictures at the end of the week.

"Bizarre? That's only half of it. It turned out that Paddy was a South African millionaire who had decided, on a whim, to become an actor. And to do it, he bought a play, hired the New Lindsay Theatre in Notting Hill for a couple of months, got himself a bunch of out-of-work rep. actors and a production team and found himself a producer — Philip Saville, now one of the top men in television.

"Paddy Orford Smith, of course, was playing the lead. And money? He spent it as if he was dying; dishing out fivers like leaves in an autumn wind. He never carried anything less than a five-pound note on him and if he wanted a packet of fags, he'd hand over a fiver and wave the change aside.

"Anyway, he liked my pictures, bought hundreds, and hired me for a month as his personal photographer at 50 quid a week And since I was the one who used to go for his cigarettes, I made about nine-pound-ten a day on the side.

"He used to have a taxi standing by on permanent hire, 24 hours a day to take him from his hotel to the theatre. I went with him everywhere, at his insistence, and I must tell you that the production of that play was something right out of an Ealing film.

"You never, I promise you, saw anything like such a shambles. I spent six years of my life in variety, but even I couldn't top that. Paddy used to walk on the stage, script in hand and stand there, booming out his lines without a clue about movement, stage presence or anything else. The rehearsals, naturally, were a scream.

"It wasn't that it was a tatty show. The play itself was bloody awful, but the production was lavish — it had to be with Paddy footing the bill. I remember once, a carpenter came up to him and said he needed a tanner's worth of nails for the scenery. Paddy just pulled out a fiver and told the bloke to get them and not worry him again.

"As the opening night drew nearer, it was clear that Paddy would never make an actor if he rehearsed until 1984 and one time at rehearsal I was so appalled I had a word with Saville.

" 'Are you really going to put this on?' I asked. 'He doesn't even know his lines.'

"Saville shrugged. 'I know. It's going to be the biggest disaster since Jutland, but what can I do? I can either quit or take the money — and I need the money.'

"I could see his point. Paddy was determined to go on and be a star, no matter who or what. The theatre was absolutely covered with pictures of him. Outside, all along the foyer walls and even inside the auditorium, everywhere you looked there were photographs of Paddy Orford Smith looking at you, posed in the sort of attitudes that went out with Irving.

"Well, I went to the opening night. Paddy still did not know his lines and couldn't even make himself up, but that didn't worry him.

"Disaster was the mildest term imaginable for that opening night. The audience heard. the whole thing twice — once from the prompter and once from Paddy. It was supposed to be a tragedy — it was in a way! — but if Paddy had been smart, he'd have made it a true comedy and it would still have been running now — like Spike Milligan's *Oblomov*. Every time he had a line to say, he'd stare into the wings until the prompt's voice floated out with his bit, and he'd boom it out, wait for someone else to say their piece, then turn again to the wings. Me, I was sick with trying not to laugh by the end of the first act.

"It was scheduled to run for three weeks, but it closed after four days. Paddy had decided he didn't want to be an actor after all, and had closed the show and sailed back to South Africa. Where he is now and what he is doing, I shudder to think.

"Anyway, when he'd gone, things at Gerrard Street settled down to normal again — I was skint!"

One thing Harrison Marks remembers vividly from this period relates to the then unknown Philip Saville. One evening in Paddy's dressing room, Saville had tried without success to interest the South African in an idea he had to produce a theatre in the round. Everyone without exception thought him slightly barmy. It is sad to think but for lack of sufficient funds and a lack of confidence in his talents, Philip Saville would have brought his ideas in this form of theatre to the British public ten years before it was eventually presented at Chichester.

All his life, Harrison Marks has been a sort of magnet for people who could properly be described as "characters". They range from the bizarre to the plain barmy. Always, but always, they turn up in extremity. This one was no exception:

Harry Sands, writer, journalist, mainly a professional soldier, but also an adventurer, circus man, fakir, busker and, above all, a gentleman, arrived on the doorstep at Gerrard Street, all five foot nothing of him.

The last time they had met was in Brighton. Then there was no current war which Sands could attend to fight in and write about so he was at a loose end.

A most deceptive fellow this Sands. Small, neat with a clipped moustache and a clipped, army officer's voice. Small, but a tough egg of the first order. A true, lethal fighting man, with a curious obsession, amounting to a passion — he was devoted to Pakistan. He adored the country, the culture and the people.

There was the time, in the pub in the arches on the front at Brighton when Harrison Marks and he were drinking with friends. Along the bar were six hefty sailors.

Suddenly Sands perked up. 'Pakistan, did I hear Pakistan mentioned?' He turned to the sailors, one of whom had made some disparaging remark.

In no time at all a heated argument was going. Harrison Marks and his companions took little notice until a sudden silence fell. The talk and clink of glasses stilled.

Only Sands' voice was to be heard. "No," he was saying, "a most offensive remark has been made. I am deeply offended. We'll go outside… this must be settled in the proper manner.

"Please, gentlemen, come outside."

The sailors looked embarrassed as they towered over him. "Forget it," said one. "You're only the size of two pennyworth of nothing."

"Forget it, Harry," his friends pleaded as well.

"I for one didn't wish to get mixed up with that hefty crew,' Harrison Marks confides. Nevertheless, Sands persisted: "Gentlemen, please, outside."

So it had to be, and so it was; they all trooped out, Harry and the sailors in a stony silence and suddenly all hell broke loose — the din was terrific. Then again silence.

"Let's go and pick him up, the idiot," said Harrison Marks.

But, to his utter shock, on the front were six very prone sailors and one erect Mr. Sands, dusting himself off.

One day, Sands announced: "I've got a fabulous job, old boy, a rigger in a circus. Great life, the circus. Should make a wonderful book."

Off he went, touring with the big-top and that was the last Harrison Marks saw of him until the day he turned up at Gerrard Street.

"I am Tumala," he declared.

"Who?"

"Tumala, the Indian fakir. I swallow swords, eat fire, stick needles through myself and lie on broken glass. And apart from that, George, I am opening in the Christmas show at the Winter Garden, and I want some pictures."

He arrived for a sitting with his gear, swords, daggers, fine needles for sticking into and through himself, broken glass, and at the studio he stripped to the waist, then started sticking the needles in.

"Half a minute, Harry," said Harrison Marks. "We'll have to get pretty close in for the pictures. I don't know how you stick those things on, but it will be pretty difficult to retouch them…"

"Stick them on," Sands burst out indignantly. "I actually do it, old boy. I actually do it. I stick them right through myself; this isn't a phoney act."

It wasn't, and to prove it on his chest were innumerable scars where the fire had dripped from the poker when he was eating it. The only precaution he took was a thin coating of Vaseline on his mouth.

"Mind over matter, old boy, that's the secret," he chirped.

Unfortunately, the show flopped, and he was out of a job.

Sitting in the studio with George one Saturday wondering what the heck to do, a busker appeared outside.

"He came every week and he was terrible," says Harrison Marks, "so I shouted: 'Wrap it up, cock, and shove off.' "

"George," Sands suddenly commanded. "That's the answer. That's it; we'll go busking. Get your banjo; we're in business. Where's a good pitch? Don't argue; I'll do the 'bottling'! Come along, old boy, let's hurry.'

Bottling is collecting the cash; ten minutes later they were in the cul-de-sac alongside Foyles bookshop. By four o'clock they had bottled £8. The bottler's job, as a sideline, is also to watch for a policeman's helmet above the heads of the crowd.

Totalling up on Sunday night they were £20 the richer.

Sands was inspired. "Think of the crowd we'd pull in if I got my gear down here," he said.

And that is how it went for the next three months. On alternate weekends Harrison Marks played and sang, the other weekends Harry did his fakir's act.

Buskers can earn good money. The famous Happy Wanderers, most of them old Music Hall pros., drive up to Town daily in their cars, park them in Newport Square and change into comic gear in a room above the fish shop.

And the famous accordionists, the little Frenchman whose pitch is around Compton and Gerrard Street, "bottles" florins and half-crowns by the dozen.

"It doesn't take many half-dollars to make a few quid an hour," Harrison Marks points out.

The public, however, is remarkably choosy. A bad busking act will starve; a good one will coin the money.

"Three months was enough," says Harrison Marks. "You know how I can't stand the cold. And it gets very chilly in the winter."

Photography was, of course, the major business. In this field Harrison Marks could make his real mark.

Success seldom happens purely by accident; there must be some underlying talent. This is what Pam had spotted and which Harrison Marks could still not fully comprehend himself. Essentially, two factors had the most important bearing on the development of his professional career.

The first was the training he had received from Percy Mumford at Universal, a master at the business who knew all there was to know about lighting and who, for the sad reasons you know, had pumped some 40 years experience into Harrison Marks' head at the time when educationalists consider a boy to be at his most receptive. It had stuck with Harrison Marks and became second nature.

The second factor was that he chose theatrical photography and from his experience of the music halls he had a deep instinctive understanding of exactly what the client was trying to express. His photographs were unique in that they interpreted and represented the customers' art and did not just display his own photographic talents.

This was why every major comedian and comic came to him. He could get right inside their acts. A comedy act is like a television set — it all shows up at the front of a flat white screen, as it were. Behind that screen, which is all that matters to the public, there is a mass of technicality. The timing, the stage directions, the pacing, the mood and tone of the act, the know-how of commanding an audience's attention. To hear comedians discussing their art can be as baffling to a layman as to listen to a nuclear scientist discussing the latest developments in his field.

One by one they came to the studio, the comics, the straight men, the rep. actors, the West End stars and slowly Harrison Marks' reputation was being established. To get the pictures his clients wanted he would soak himself into their parts, watching their acts or plays until he had completely absorbed the atmosphere.

Bela Lugosi arrived from America to tour in the role he created for the cinema in 1931, Count Dracula. Harrison Marks was asked to do the pictures.

"I had admired this man for years," he says. "It was really the most exciting commission. I had seen the old film, but I had never seen him live.

"I went down to Brighton to watch him and I sat through the matinee and the evening performance before going backstage to meet him.

"It was an astonishing performance when he made his entrance through the French windows up-stage it was fantastic and dramatic. He really looked as if he had just flown down from his castle across the valley and landed that instant at the window.

"When I met him he was a quiet and sweet and charming man. But he lived for this part. He'd played it for 30 years.

"I was going to shoot the stuff at the Lewisham Hippodrome and the next time I met him was round there. I arrived early, about six o'clock. I found him in full make-up an hour-and-a-half before curtain up.

"In a trance, he was sitting in front of his mirror with his hands outstretched to the dressing table. His piercing eyes were staring into the mirror. Quite honestly, he looked as if he was a vampire — for real 1 He didn't move an inch.

"His wife was there, and she was a darling. 'Quiet,' she whispered. 'Mr. Lugosi never speaks to a soul for at least an hour before the performance. He sits and soaks in the part and the mood; we mustn't disturb him.'

"Dracula was their lives. On her jacket there was an enormous diamond brooch in the shape of a bat and he wore a ring with the Dracula coat of arms. There is an actual Dracula family, and he had got permission from them to use the coat of arms.

"One of the fascinating things about him was the deep Dracula accent he had — he spoke exactly the same off stage as he did when playing the part. At our first meeting I had been chatting with him for about half-an-hour in my native London-type accent when he suddenly swung round in his chair and thundered in that deep, rolling voice: 'Vat is dis man sayinck? I don't oonderstant von word off it

Stars there were in plenty but, not unexpectedly, there were, too, the oddballs.

"This chap turned up one morning, a real old queen with a wide brimmed hat and a flowing cape; he looked a real, old Shakespearian ham. 'My boy,' he drawled. 'I want you to take some photographs, very special photographs,' and he paused dramatically and added meaningfully '...in costume.'

"So I clicked on; I thought he's a drag act. 'Sure,' I said, 'when do you want them?'

"...be round tomorrow,' he didn't so much say it as declaim it. Next day he turned up in a taxi with three trunks. We're in for some session here, I thought, with all this gear; he'll keep me going all day. I put him in the changing room and after about three-quarters-of-an-hour, I asked him how long he'd be. 'Some time yet, laddy, some time yet. So I said

I'd get on with some work in the dark room and would he ring the bell as soon as he was ready.

"Well, two hours later, the bell rang. I went up.

"Honestly, it was the make-up which got me first. It was startling. First of all he had a tatty, frowsy blonde wig (bright yellow), black false eyelashes about an inch long, the rouge on his cheeks stood out like target centres, mascara and lipstick — he had ladled it on.

"Perched on top of all this was an enormous Ascot picture hat. Round his neck was a black silk band with a medallion hanging from it. He was wearing long black gloves, a suspender-belt and long black stockings. That was all. He was posing with a parasol; his nose stuck up in the air in what he thought was an elegant stance.

"I gasped… dumbstruck for about 20 seconds; for this poor devil was neither one thing nor the other. He had the sagging breasts of a middle-aged woman… and below, the genitals of a very well developed man. I recovered my composure… 'What the hell… I'm not going to take pictures of you like that!' He wilted and pleaded that he only wanted a few personal pictures and he wasn't concerned about the price. 'Look chum,' I said, 'you took two bloody hours to put that lot on; I'll give you two minutes to get your clothes on .. . and out.' He was out of that studio, dressed, with all his baggage in one minute flat.

"I rushed to the door and there wasn't a sign of him. If he had gone on the boards, he could have had a better act than Houdini."

Nude photography can, and does, attract many unsavoury characters, like the two who have approached Harrison Marks on several occasions.

They arrived at the studio and asked to see some "interesting pictures". It became clear that they were looking for pornography and they put a proposition to him.

"Look," they said. "You've got the set-up here, why waste it? We'll provide the models, all you have to do is to shoot the sets of pictures. We'll pay you 500, in notes, before you do the job — it's simple." And they added the rider that they were prepared to pay £500 a week.

They were turned down flat. Even though they pressed the issue several times.

It is a singular thought, however, that a set of dirty pictures should be worth so much. What can the total value of the market be at that price?

Businesslike and exacting these people can be, too; now, apparently, they are aiming at quality control. After Harrison Marks' success in films some time later, they came back in 1966 and pleaded with him to make blue films.

"This stuff we get from the Continent is substandard," they explained. "We've got to get quality. Our customers don't like all the badly lit, out of focus trash that comes in from abroad. They're getting very discerning; they want good production and camera work. If you put your talents to it, we could clean up on the worldwide market 1 "

Harrison Marks replied: "If I wasn't interested when I was broke 14 years ago, why on earth should I be interested now? I don't want anything AT ALL to do with it."

"Come now, Mr. Marks," said the leader of the deputation, "we know you're rich, but even you must be interested in £2,000 a week, in cash, no tax, no questions."

Harrison Marks wasn't, isn't and never will be.

It is incredibly difficult to break this racket and the police are almost at a dead end. Even though the set-up is transparent, to nail any group or single person is exceptionally complicated.

If a photographer or filmmaker falls into the trap, immediately he is subjected to blackmail and his money rapidly dries up.

How can he complain to the police without incriminating himself? The operators are far too wide to walk into a police trap, say, when a film is being made. The chances are that the film man never knows who is behind it.

If you call the police when you are being propositioned, how do you prove it? More important, how do the police prove it? Usually the only people who get nabbed are the exhibitors or the producers who are caught red-handed. And often they have been "set-up" for falling out of line.

There was one amusing incident in 1966 which was told in court with some irony.

An old Soho lag, fresh from Wormwood Scrubs that very morning and short of money, looked up his old cronies. They were running a blue show in Soho. "There's a tenner," they said." Get round the parish and drum up some business. We want them about 45, well off and unattached. But make sure they've got plenty of brass and are good spenders."

Some hours later he telephoned. “Got a sitter here,” he said. “He’s stacked. Been on the piss all day and he keeps ringing his missus to say he’s been delayed. He’s dead keen.”

A perfect set-up. “Marvellous,” said the blue men. “Wheel him in, you’ll get your cut. Don’t bring him down direct. Get him a bit lost so he can’t pinpoint the place.”

So they waltzed around the back-doubles and arrived in the nick of time for the second house.

The door opened and faces fell. “You screaming nit! “the blue men said to the lag. “This is the deputy chief of the vice squad! “

Unfortunate old lag, he was back behind bars 13 hours and 20 minutes after leaving the Scrubs.

CHAPTER 9

Pam Again

ALL this time Pam, of course, was the rock anchor. As solid, as compatible and as loyal when the money gushed in as she had been on — or below — the breadline. The money just did not affect her but it devastated Harrison Marks, as he tells

"It was I who went mad with the stuff. She never asked for anything at all while I was running around spending like I had only one day left to live. I bought yachts, houses, cars, clothes, jewellery — anything to be had for money; I wanted it.

"It wasn't by any means, entirely selfish. My real joy, the greatest pleasure I had was giving things to Pam. I gave her a fur coat which cost £4,500, not because it cost so much, but only because it was the best that money could buy and I honestly felt that she deserved it.

"But it was the day I bought her a wristwatch that I got involved in one of the most amusing incidents I can remember.

"I had promised myself and Pam that I would get her a really superb wristwatch. We looked at dozens together, but none were quite what she wanted and nothing I saw was up to the standard I had set for this special gift, and I kept on looking.

"Now, it so happened one day, that I had to rush from my studio to the Kodak supply shop in Regent Street. I had to go in the middle of a session for some reason and I was dressed in my usual working costume of old slacks, slippers, a sports shirt and a stained sweater. Certainly, I did not look very special. Anyway, dashing up Regent Street, I passed Garrards, the world-famous jewellers, and glanced in the window. They had put on a most magnificent showcase. I remember it clearly — a green velvet drape in the middle of which stood about three items, one of which was the most magnificent bracelet I have ever clapped eyes on. It was in the form of a snake, exquisitely worked in gold with its head studded with diamonds and rubies. It was quite superb.

“I had not time to stop at that moment, however, and hurried on to Kodak’s. But on the way back, I stopped again and looked in the jeweller’s window. I was fascinated by the snake bracelet and I dearly wanted to get it for Pam, so I went into the shop. “Of course, I forgot that I was dressed like a beatnik. Otherwise I should not have been surprised to see the look of horror which flickered for a second across the face of the assistant who met me at the counter.

“Yes, sir,” he enquired — no doubt thinking I had come to empty the dustbins.

“That snake bracelet in the window,” I said. “I’d like to see it.’

“That shook him. ‘I beg your pardon?’

“The snake bracelet. I’d like to see it.”

“Well, I was going to play it out, but I had to feel sorry for the poor assistant. Much though he would like to have thrown me out in the street, I should think, he had to maintain the dignity of the place and although he paled when I again asked to see the establishment’s prize piece, he couldn’t very well refuse. But as he moved away towards the window, I saw him have a quick word with another bloke and they both shot me a glance heavy with suspicion. At the same time, the serjeant on the door moved inside and stood weightily between me and the street!

“Anyway, he brought it out, and it was truly beyond description. It had come from the personal collection of the deposed King Farouk of Egypt. And whatever else the old boy had, he sure had taste. It was a beautiful piece of jewellery — and what’s more, I found that the head of the snake snapped open to reveal a wristwatch. That was it.

“ ‘How much is it?’ I asked.

‘The assistant drew himself up to deliver the knock-out — you could see it. Two thousand, eight hundred pounds… sir!’

“I nodded. ‘Good,’ I said. ‘I’d like to bring my wife down to see it.’

“And that, they must have thought, was the last we’ll see of that tramp.

“However, I hurried home to get Pam in a hurry. I found her at the easel, painting and, if anything, she looked even more dishevelled than I did, but there was no time to change so we hopped a cab and returned to Regent Street.

“The look on the face of the same assistant when

I came back with Pam, in her flat shoes, old slacks and sweater was one of sheer disbelief. You've seen an actor do a double-take? Well, that's exactly what this bloke did.

"This time, when he got the bracelet out there were at least two men between us and the door and when Pam slipped it on her wrist, he went a shade paler than ever.

"Pam, of course, fell in love with the thing as I hoped she would.

"Right," I told the assistant. "I'll have it!" "What?" he croaked.

"I'll have it," I said. "Two thousand, eight hundred, wasn't it?" And I fished out my chequebook.

"When I handed him the cheque, his nerve went completely. He said something about getting the sale authorised and almost ran into the back room somewhere. I knew very well he was going to phone my bank and it was obvious he did for when he came back, he was a different man. He was smiling, he wanted to know if we wanted it gift-wrapped or delivered and heaven knows what else.

"The thing about Pam and I," says Harrison Marks, "is that we saw eye-to-eye on everything. It was a swinging affair all the time. There can never be another Pam, as long as I live.

"We shared everything. Come to think of it; it was really quite remarkable.

"It wasn't, for instance, that we both liked weekends in the country, but we both liked exactly the same places in the country. We'd get to one spot and without saying a word, we would know instinctively if we were both happy.

"It was the same with people and things. And we worked together in complete harmony. That may have been one of the causes for the break-up.

"All the millions of people who have looked at pictures of Pam just cannot realise what was behind this woman. I told you, she was a very talented painter, she was also a wonderful classical pianist, really up to professional standard.

"When we had expanded and taken over all the premises in Gerrard Street, we moved our flat to Hampstead.

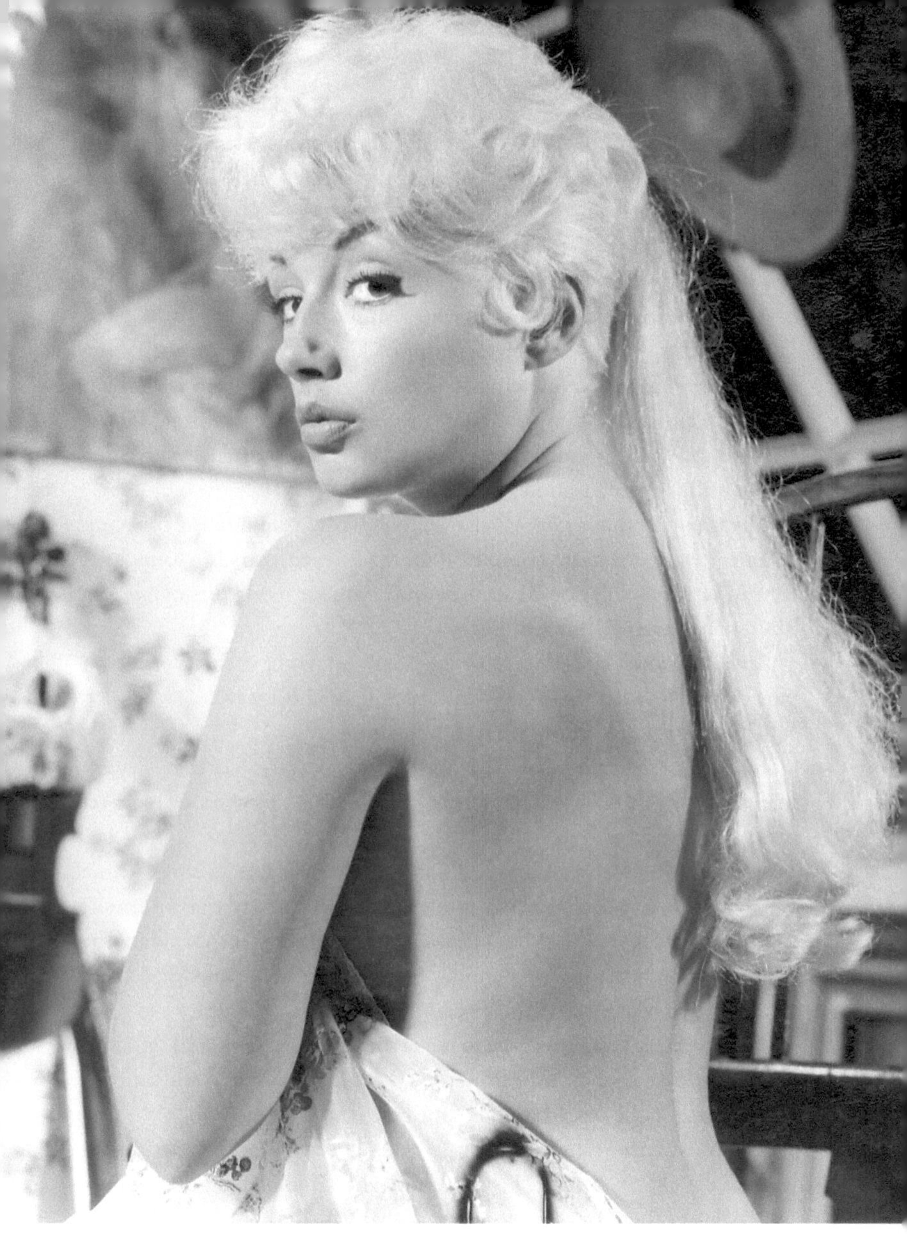

The incomparable Pamela Green

"Every single morning of our lives together up there, she was up with me and at 9 o'clock we left together for the studio. She had no need to do it but she just did.

"It went on for seven years like that, and in the whole of that time I was faithful to her. Of all men in London, I must have had quite the most temptation and by far the greatest opportunities.

"Remember, when I'm photographing women, I was not just taking snapshots; I am portraying emotions and I get very involved with them.

"Really, a woman's body does nothing for me. I go, every time, for the face. To me, it is the most important facet of any woman, everything she is, or hopes to be, shows in her face.

"It was one woman's face which eventually led, I think, to the break-up.

"But it was a lot more complex than that. Seven years is a long, long time in retrospect. It doesn't seem so when you are living through it, but it is a considerable chunk of life.

And it is time enough to grow together and to get to know a person, particularly if you are as deeply in love as Pam and I were.

"This was the situation. We had everything.

Every material thing we could ever wish for plus the fact that we were free to do what we wished, go where we wanted — to work or play. Yet something was missing.

"You can only drive in one Rolls at a time or eat one meal at a time. When you've got it all, well, it would be foolish to say that it doesn't matter anymore, it does; but it loses its dominating importance, the compelling urgency to make money and a living disappears. Ideas and the ability to create new things become far more important.

"For instance, I had this urge to make movies and I sank £80,000 into one — my own money. If I had wanted, I could have retired and sat back in comfort for the rest of my life, but that is by the way.

"The most important thing in my life had been meeting Pam, leaving her was equally important. Just how and why it happened I do not fully understand. There were no rows, no disagreements. We were, and still are, the best of pals; we were never bored with each other. It was, in fact, a slow erosion.

"Take all the factors; we had money, far too much money — and that's a fact. Yet something was missing.

"I felt it in tiny ways. I began to resent her getting up with me in the morning and coming to the studio. We would go home together every night; everything would be perfect at the flat; obviously we could afford to pay for the best help. Yet the place seemed empty. It didn't feel like a home and I began to think, it shouldn't be like this. The place should feel lived in; there should be somebody waiting here to welcome me when I come home at night. It was a silly feeling, completely irrational — almost the suburban man creeping through the Bohemian exterior. Nevertheless, the feeling was there.

"But Pam couldn't give up the studio. For the first time a barrier had grown up between us. It wasn't a clearly defined thing, but that instantaneous, telepathic communication between us was dying. It's one of those things; you don't really know it's there until it's gone. For the first time I'd find myself asking: 'I wonder what Pam will feel about this or that?' or 'I wonder what she's thinking?' I'd never had to do that before.

"In turn, I could feel that she was becoming edgy and discontented. Nothing direct was ever said, and bear in mind that this was happening over a period of time.

"And I think she was getting a little jealous. She was only 32, but she began to disapprove of the models and she became hyper-critical of some of them. She would look at a girl and say: 'I can't possibly imagine what you can see in her,' and things like that. She had never done that before, and it was very disconcerting.

"Eventually, a woman did cause the final break. Which might be a very common occurrence, but in my case is rather ironic.

"Every Easter Pam and I had gone to Holland to visit her people, usually we stayed for three weeks. I always enjoyed it enormously.

"This year I was up to the eyes in work at the studio. The work just had to be done. So I said, 'Look, Pam — you go over by yourself and have a good time; you need a break. And it will do us both a power of good to be away from each other for a time.

"That was it, quite simply. There was no ulterior motive of any kind. Pam was reluctant, but she knew how much work we had on hand, so she agreed and off she went.

"For a couple of weeks I got stuck into the job. I went home by myself in the evening and took myself off to see the odd picture.

“At the time, I had a girl working for me, a very very beautiful girl, who was the image of Marilyn Monroe. She wasn’t a model; she was my secretary. All I had ever done was to talk to her in the office; I had never been out with her. She was a very reserved sort of girl. Quiet, she’d just recently been divorced.

“One night I was going to see the film ‘Rob Roy’. ‘Why don’t you come?’ I suggested. She said: ‘I don’t really think I should.’ I pressed the point, more than anything I wanted a companion. I hate sitting in a cinema by myself. ‘Oh, come along,’ I argued. ‘What possible harm can there be in it? We’re just going to the flicks… you’ve known me long enough.’

“Well, she agreed. We saw the film, had a spot of dinner and we dropped back to the flat for a couple of drinks. She was a very, very nice girl. Tremendously intelligent, really easy to get along with. But she was still very reserved.

“How it ever happened, to this day I do not know. But suddenly it all happened and it started a tempestuous affair.

“But all the time I kept telling myself, ‘watch it, George, you’re in love with Pam, she’s a really wonderful person.’

“And the girl knew Pam as well. We were both really reluctant. We became so deeply involved and so desperately in love it was agony.

She couldn’t stay at the studio and I couldn’t bear to be without her for more than a couple of hours. I used to wonder where she was, if she was away. And I would think the most terrible thoughts. In fact, I could think of nothing else but her. Everything else seemed to be happening in a haze — it all had a dream-like quality.

“I really went over the top. I set her up in a flat and I completely rearranged my days so that I could be with her. I worked out all my times so that I could get round to the flat as often as possible, which was damned nearly all the time.

“What a situation; the more I loved this girl, the more aware I grew of Pam. I couldn’t bear to hurt Pam. I passionately didn’t want to hurt her.

“But I was so much in love with the girl that eventually the inevitable happened. She became pregnant.

“What on earth to do? Suddenly, everything clarified. All my doubts disappeared; that feeling of discontent I’d had for a year just went. I knew this was the answer. 'Have the child,' I said. 'We'll get this lot sorted out.' Everything now seemed simple; I thought I had found the answer. Was I wrong! The next fortnight is burned into my memory.

"Now, the first thing I did every morning when I got to the studio was to telephone the flat. This morning there was no reply. I didn't worry much. But I kept on trying. Still no reply. It was only a couple of hours, but it was very curious — we were never out of touch with each other for more than a couple of hours at the most.

"I had a meeting that morning. It seemed to drag on forever. It was an age before I could wrap it up and shoot down to the flat.

"No one there. I waited. She didn't come. I waited, getting more and more frantic. Still, she didn't come — and not a word.

"I was nearly mad. I rushed round to every haunt where I thought she might be. Nobody had seen her. Soon as I got into one place, I thought I might have missed her at the other. I screamed round and round, backwards and forwards between everywhere we'd ever been. I telephoned every single person who had ever known her or us.

"I got used to the terrible drop in spirits every time I called back at the flat and it was empty.

"She had disappeared completely off the face of the earth.

"Then the most appalling, terrifying thoughts crept in. Over and over again I told myself: 'She wouldn't do that, she wouldn't.' The doubt persisted. I tried to kill it. 'She wouldn't, she couldn't; we were far, far, far too deeply in love.

"It went on for a full fortnight. Day in day out. Touring the haunts, telephoning everybody. Making those awful, dreadful checks with what we call the authorities.

"Fourteen days later she walked back into the flat.

" 'I've been away to the country,' she said. 'I didn't tell you, because you would have stopped me. I've had an abortion.'

"I was stupified, bowled over, utterly shattered. I couldn't even ask why.

"Then she said: 'I thought it would be the best thing for you.'

"I never asked the reasoning. I didn't question her. My mind was just blank incomprehension.

"Later, I looked at Pam, and the first bitter thought — the only bitter thought I have ever had about her — came into my mind. It was unfair;

I was ashamed of it. I thought: 'You have everything and you won't give me the one thing I really want.' It was bitter and I was bitterly ashamed of thinking it.

"There were no rows; we had a calm discussion; there were no recriminations; we remained friends. We decided we were becoming a little bored with each other living together day and night. A three months separation would be good for us both.

"It was the end. A perfect union had outlived its time. We never went back together. We had fallen out of love.

"At the end there was a bitter irony. Just before Pam and I split, the girl took a job with a touring dance band and left London… and me. A couple of years went by before we met quite by accident in a club. She had by this time married the pianist in the band and I am glad to say was very happy with him. It was, however, a rather beautiful, but sad evening talking of old times and mulling over what might have been…

CHAPTER 10

Moment of Parting

SO Pamela went and the wild years began. But the new life of unbridled freedom started in curiously contradictory terms. The day Pam walked out of the flat for the last time, Harrison Marks experienced a feeling of release and freedom and of being, for the first time, his own master, not exactly with only himself to consider, but certainly emotionally untrammelled. But why?

He had, in fact, previously achieved as great a degree of freedom as is humanly possible in as much that anything he wanted, he could have. The relationship with Pam fulfilled most of the conditions they both required. There was no animosity and still there was great mutual affection.

Sadly, the answer, as we said before, was money. By this time they should have been used to it. They weren't. They allowed it to corrupt a splendid relationship and to tarnish affection in the most insidious way of all — by inducing boredom.

The decision to separate was taken late one evening just before going to bed. There was a calm discussion; they had never quarrelled since the first day they met, and they were determined not to mar that record by fighting on their last night together.

Harrison Marks did not know what he really wanted. He only knew that to find it he would have to be apart from Pam. During the previous years they had gradually become strangers, eating, sleeping, loving and working together, but no longer finding in one another the deep joy that had gone with the earlier years.

They had lost touch; there was no longer the almost telepathic communication they had shared since they had first met.

The fact that it was almost impossible to put a finger on the root of the trouble was as distressing as any single factor in the situation.

George had suggested a separation. It was going to be temporary — a few weeks apart to sort things out and then everything as before.

But in his heart, he knew when Pam walked out of the flat that morning it was for the last time. It was a day of sadness and puzzlement — and relief.

Earlier, before breakfast, Pam had telephoned her parents to tell them that she would be spending a few weeks at home.

They had no idea that the marriage was breaking up. But once again they were really wonderful. There were no recriminations, nor was any unwanted advice profferred. They were sad but compassionate. For years after, Harrison Marks was a regular visitor to the Green home in West Wickham. There was never any embarrassment when he visited them for Sunday lunch. But, though it was never mentioned, he knew that they were unhappy he and Pam could no longer make a go of it.

How many worlds separate the concept and the actuality? And how wide is the gap between discussion and the fulfilment?

There came the ultimate moment of parting. The door slammed and, just as a railway station platform becomes the loneliest place in the world when the train bearing a loved one pulls out, so the flat was filled with emptiness.

Always it had lacked something, and now that missing homeliness became too, too apparent — silence and bareness, familiar objects missing, and utter wretchedness and loneliness.

There was an urge to rush after Pam and call her back. It was far too late for that.

Though, at the same time, overshadowing all his other feelings, was one of complete relief.

"After living with someone for eight years shock and loneliness were inevitable," he says. "We had loved each other like mad, and we had a tremendous time together. I told you, we liked the same music, the same plays, the same films; in fact, the same everything. A wonderful partnership. Perhaps, too wonderful. I don't know."

Single thinking is hard to return to after a length of time during which you have automatically considered someone else. Nearly all divorcees find it a difficult adjustment to make; they have been subconsciously conditioned to thinking for two, or more, and it requires a conscious act of judgment to revert to a single state of mind.

In those eight years, he had made no plans that did not include her. But this had all changed. Now he wanted time; free time, to think the whole thing out.

He remembers thinking "Thank God" after she left. There was no dislike of her, just an overwhelming happiness that he was finally on his own again.

But to be free and alone was not really what he wanted. It was not in the nature of the man. Basically a social character, even a distinctly gregarious one in the way that some "non-organisation" men who prefer to go it alone in business quite often are, one suspects that Harrison Marks found a mental blockage in solitariness.

Simply, he needed someone to talk to. There was, as always, a ready ear. And this ear was also seeking sympathy. Two people in emotional trouble and a sentimental wilderness, two souls seeking solace: it was a natural — it had to happen.

The woman was Dawn, a former model who had over the years became a close friend.

Two days before the break-up with Pam the girl had telephoned George. She badly needed a shoulder to cry on.

For three years she had been carrying on a passionate affair with a married man. He had two sons at college and had promised her that when they were old enough he would leave his wife and marry her. George had warned her what the probable outcome of their association would be, but of course, she had not listened.

Eventually it had happened. The man had tired of Dawn and suddenly announced one day that everything was over between them.

"She poured out her troubles, and I gave her the sympathy I knew she needed. But I didn't realise that in a couple of days I would be doing the crying, and she would be ladling out the kind words. "When Pam left I called Dawn and said, Now it's my turn.' "

That night he needed her friendship more than ever before — quite desperately in fact. But he had no intention of starting an affair.

"Something terrible has happened to me, too," I told her. "We'd better drown our sorrows in a bottle tonight. What do you think?"

" 'A good idea,' she agreed. But purely as mates."

That was just the way George wanted it. For him, there was to be no marching up and down Piccadilly shouting "Whoopee, now I'm free." Not for him a grab at the first available woman to celebrate his newly achieved status. Let it all happen gradually, he decided. To be sure it did.

So the sad, sad spree began. The talk, the consoling, the forgetting went on for four days and four nights. The day's expiation culminated nightly in the 55 Room, in Jermyn Street, and the drink flowed until the world became rose-coloured again — for the time being.

They were good for each other — and each of them was also good for a hell of a hangover the following morning — but the glow of companionship kept them warm each evening.

Suddenly, in the middle of the night, George felt that Dawn deserved flowers. It was 3 o'clock in the morning, but no problem. Along the route home was a shining, newly-completed office building and outside was a concrete trough brimming with hydrangeas. So George stopped the car and presented an armful to Dawn.

She was touched, visibly touched.

So each succeeding night as they staggered to the car they would stop and carefully uproot an armful of blooms.

"The bloody car was full of the things every morning," says George. "I didn't know what to do with them, so I ended up presenting them to my mother.

"Before the week was out she had a garden full of hydrangeas and the concrete trough was empty."

Within a few weeks, George had given up all thoughts of attempting a reconciliation with Pam. Marriage, he decided, was just not for him.

Not that he wanted to sever his connection with Pam completely. For three years after their separation, Pam continued to model for him at his studio.

She is a director and shareholder in two of his companies which gives her financial security and independence.

"What happened to force us apart was a very personal thing between us. But how can I ever forget the help she gave me in those early days. Without that, I probably wouldn't be in the position I am in today."

So, sadly, drunkenly and in remorse the wild years started, the years of womanising, socialising and generally living it up were now, as it were, officially declared open. The latent playboy in Harrison Marks emerged; zestful, lustful, almost insatiable — now not only were women good to look at, they were even better to taste. Absolved from emotional responsibility, he became totally irresponsible in love.

Seduction, in his particular circumstances, he discovered was comparatively simple. He couldn't leave it at that, though, far, far too simple. No, he had to keep falling in love. Apart from any physical consideration, the emotional exhaustion must have been excessive. Within Harrison Marks there is a seething energy wiggling away like a tape-worm. It has to break out in some direction or other; it has to enthuse over something. Usually it is work or women, and since women are his work he is caught in an ever-tightening circle.

Life doesn't stand still, nor does business and the second stage of the Harrison Marks career was approaching. He didn't at first recognise it, in fact, he tried to reject it.

For two years he had been making films in a small way. He was turning out home movies, ten-minute shorts featuring nudes, and children's comedy.

One day two men called at the studio without an appointment. They wanted him, they said, to make a full-length feature film. And to help him they were willing to put up half the money.

"They wanted to know if I had seen any of the nudist films which were doing the rounds in the London art cinemas. I hadn't. And as they sat and talked to me about their plans I found myself asking 'what the hell do I know about film production?'

"The answer to that was a straight 'nothing.' I was a technician and knew what I was supposed to be doing. If I had been put in an editing room I would have been able to edit, and I also knew a little about sound and a great deal about cameras.

"But I didn't know about production. And these men were talking in terms of twenty thousand pounds. I couldn't see why I should risk it."

If anyone can make a feature film about nudism, you can, the two men argued. You have the name and reputation as being the best nude photographer in the country.

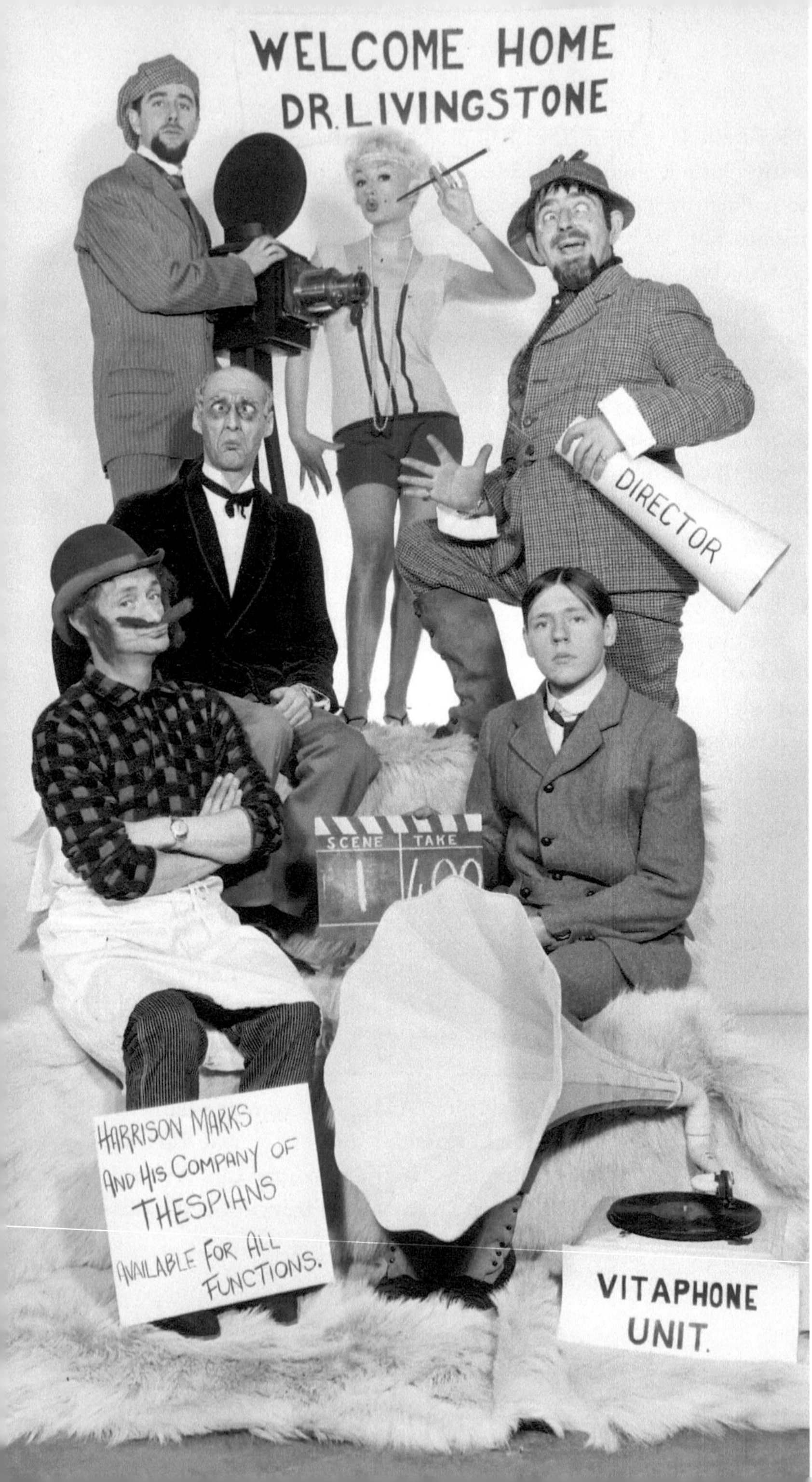

WELCOME HOME
DR. LIVINGSTONE
DIRECTOR
SCENE TAKE
1 400
HARRISON MARKS
AND HIS COMPANY OF
THESPIANS
AVAILABLE FOR ALL
FUNCTIONS.
VITAPHONE
UNIT.

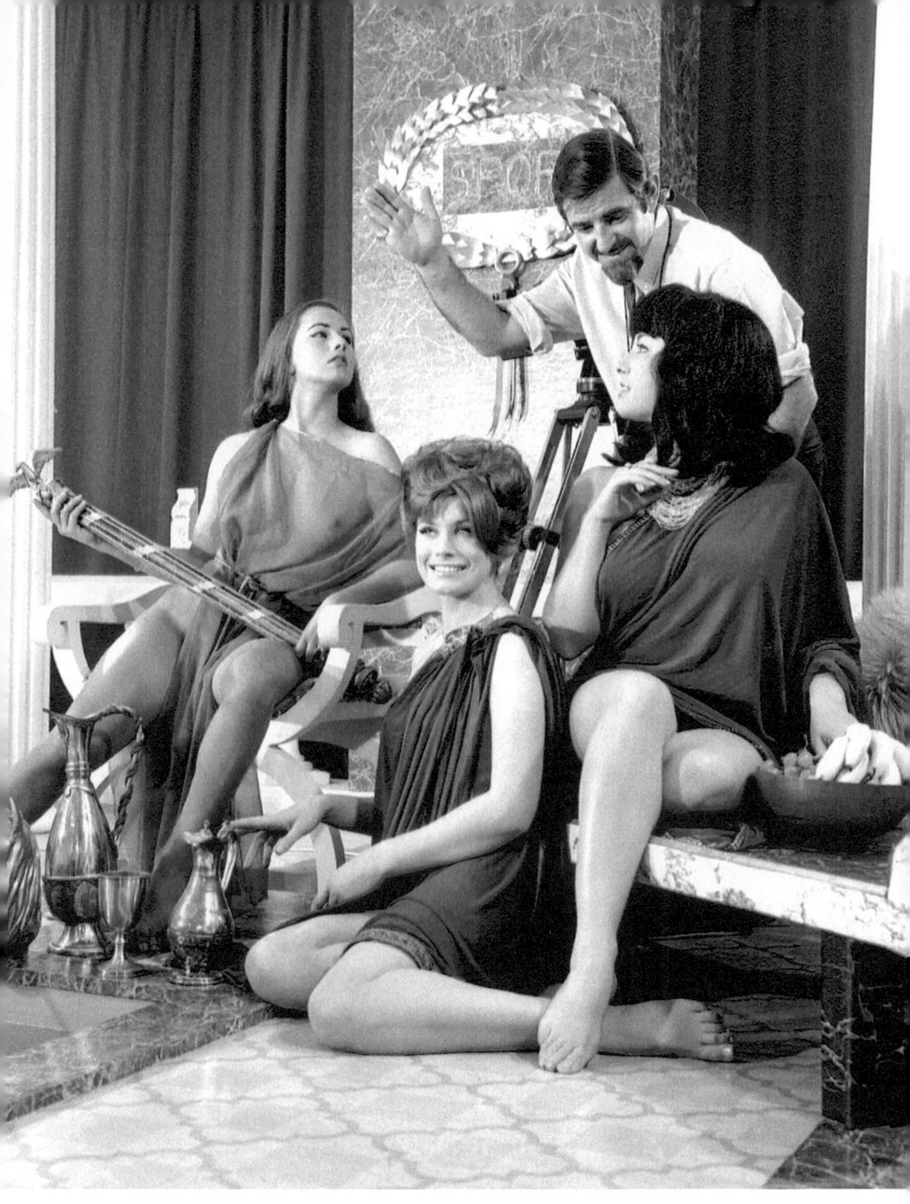

Above: George Harrison Marks directing a scence with Marina Jones, Dawn Grayson and June Palmer

Right: Right: You don't have to be mad to work for George Harrison Marks, but it helps!

But for once he was unsure of himself. He did not want to get involved in a business he knew so little about. Firmly but politely he turned down their offer.

For more than three months they pushed the idea. But he refused to consider it. Pushing the point to its extremes, they took him to a lavish lunch in one of London's most exclusive restaurants, washed down with quantities of fine old claret. After the meal, they announced that they were taking him to the cinema. Not a regular show but a special private run through of two current nudist films.

They had booked a preview cinema in Wardour Street and would not take no for an answer.

"You've eaten lunch, and now you've of to sit down and watch films," they announced. "After that, we can talk."

They ran the two films through and to Harrison Marks they seemed so incredibly poor that he immediately told them "If I couldn't make better than those then I would give the whole racket up."

"In that case, you'd better make one," they told him.

Again he hesitated. The standard of photography of the girls in the films he had just seen was terrible. They were just rubbish. But could he do any better?

Well, he certainly couldn't do any worse he decided and agreed there and then to go ahead. "I'll make these things look like amateur movies by the time I've finished," he told them. "When do I get started?"

That afternoon they discussed just what kind of a picture he would make.

It had to be about naturism as this was the only way in which a film could get past the censor. He is governed by certain rules which state that only authentic naturists can be shown on the big screen for general release.

The script was started that same evening, and the film "Naked as Nature Intended" was destined to be a smash hit, playing for fifteen months to packed houses.

Writing the script and handling the arrangements for going on location, in fact getting back to real work, helped to disperse the last lingering memories of marriage.

Although he had already decided there could be no returning to Pam, the habits of years persisted. For instance, he found it difficult not to rush away when the clock in a night club said after midnight.

"What the hell am I doing out. I should be home," he would think. But there was no reason for going home. No-one was there to ask him why he had stayed out so late or who he had been with.

The story, George decided, would be about a group of girls going on holiday. They would be from different walks of life and individually would go right the way down through Devon and Cornwall eventually winding up at a nudist camp where they would all meet.

During this journey through the West Country their paths would cross repeatedly. But though they often passed within a few feet of one another they would not meet.

It was to be a very pretty film, in fact, a good type of travelogue. But all this dosed with a hefty helping of showmanship and glamour.

There would not be a nude sequence in it until twenty-five minutes before the end. The interest would be kept going purely by using the girls. They were very beautiful, and George decided that was all that was needed.

Even in ordinary filming, finding locations is difficult enough. For a nude film the problems multiply. Always one must be careful about offending public taste and decency, and one must also avoid peeping Toms.

Harrison Marks had done a great deal of location work in Cornwall. He knew how difficult it was to find suitable places sufficiently secluded even for a small stills unit. A whole film unit would be very tough to handle and conceal.

Previously there had been the odd spot of trouble — like the time when they were working on a private estate well away from the beaten track. They noticed an old Morris parked on the road at a spot overlooking the location. Usually, at times like this, the location manager wanders over to the intruder and chats him or her up, and explains just what is going on. Most people are remarkably cooperative.

On this occasion, there was no co-operation at all. An elderly gentleman was behind the wheel, and he proved to be as bristly as his moustache.

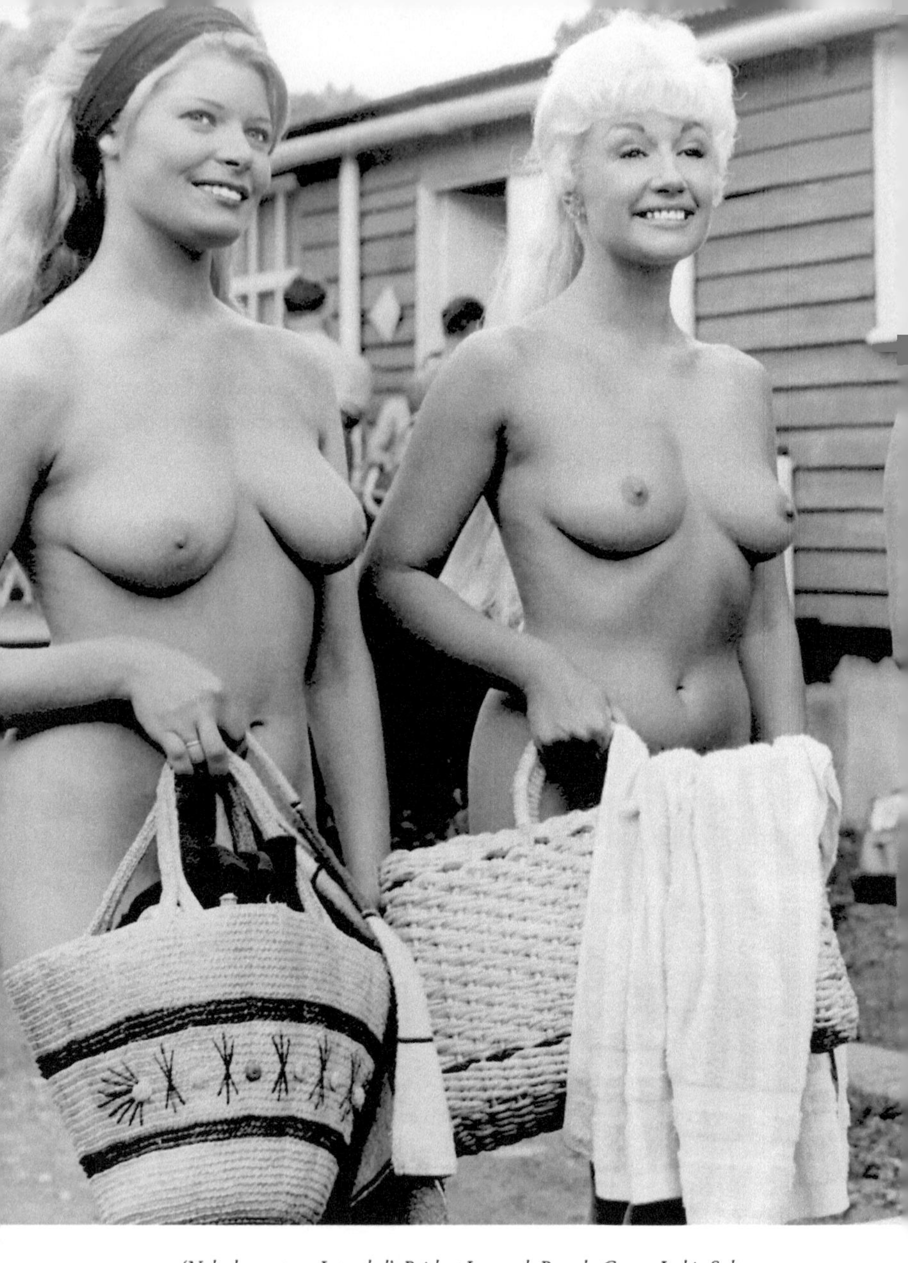

'Naked as nature Intended': Bridget Leonard, Pamela Green, Jackie Salt and Petrina Forsyth — towels at the ready to keep the censors happy

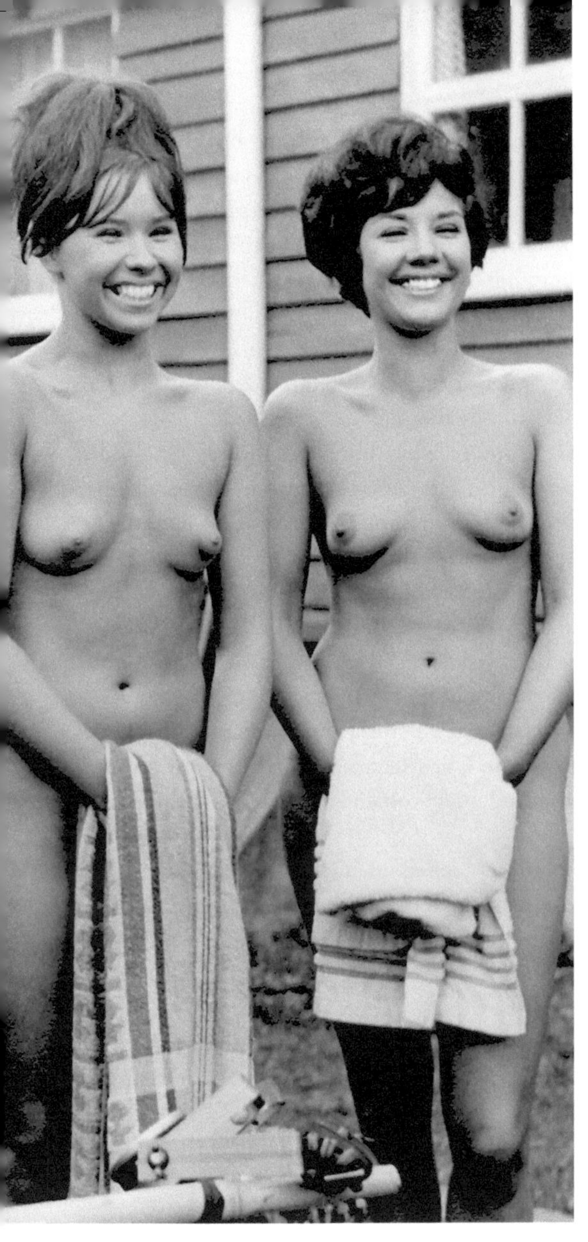

Tony, the manager, started to say what was going on when the old fellow exploded. His face went purple, his eyes popped and he bellowed: "I knew it, I knew it — you're taking phonographic photographs (the word was his). Filth, besmirching the fair name of British womanhood, corrupting the innocent minds of youth, degrading marriage, desecrating woman's sacred rights." He had the lot.

Tony called George over. He couldn't get a word in. "I've caught you at it, you filthy phonographers, caught you red-handed," the old man screeched. There was no calming him down.

Harrison Marks said: "Tony, take the number of this car," and added, "Look, Sir, you have just made a very serious allegation concerning pornography. If you won't give me your name, I'll trace it through the car and my solicitors will be in touch with you.

"Actually, I didn't intend to do anything," he explains, "I just wanted to shut the old boy up and calm him down. But could I? — oh, dear me, no."

"Filth. filth, filth," he bellowed. "Naked women in the woods. Orgies. I've caught you. I'm going straight for the police."

"Eventually he shoved off. The car went down the road in a series of jerks like an old Keystone Cops sequence, with the old boy still howling about obscenities and nude women besmirching the fair county of Cornwall.

"Then, about an hour later, I looked up, and spotted another car just passing the gap in the hedge where the old boy had stopped. It didn't appear on the rise of the hill a little further up and a couple of minutes later it backed down to the gap.

"So I said: 'Cover-up, girls, we've got more visitors.'

"We usually did that as soon as strangers were spotted. Then I took a close look at the car. It was a Wolseley and out of it were climbing two figures in familiar uniforms and flat hats.

The old boy had been as good as his word and notified the police.

Consider the policeman's position. They were as embarrassed as we were. From the word go they were sympathetic and of course they had to be very careful. They realised that they couldn't, as public officials, go around making wild allegations that the old boy had done. Any policeman hesitates before using the word pornographic — its implications are very serious. Later they said that immediately they saw us they realised that we were professional people. But they had received a complaint, and they had to investigate.

If anything I was a little techy at yet another interruption to the day's work. They proved to be a couple of very nice blokes.

"Slowly they meandered down the track toward our location, very much taking their time. They approached us as they might approach an erring driver they'd pulled up. One came straight to me, the other walked slowly round the set-up, eyeing the props and clothes and things.

"Silence. Then one said, 'Well then, what's going on here… or should I say rather what's coming off?'

" 'Look, officer,' I said, 'we're taking pictures for a London magazine, my girls are working in the nude, and they're shy. They don't like being watched by strangers.'

" 'We've had one old nut-case here already today who spent his time making serious allegations.'

The policeman suddenly wiped the smile from his face. 'You know you're on private property,' he queried, 'have you got permission?' 'Of course I've got permission,' I was getting a little tart myself. 'And come to think of it, that silly old devil was in fact trespassing when he parked where he did…

"The policeman looked a little quizzical. 'Yes,' he said, perhaps he was…

"Then I said, 'Look, officer, whatever you may have been told today, there is nothing going on here, nothing AT ALL except taking art studies.' I pointed to the Hasselblads, Rollies and the Linhof and said, 'I don't go carting around two or three thousand quids worth of stuff just to fix up a poking party. If you want to check my credentials, go and see Colonel… (I mentioned the owner of the estate). He knows all about it and exactly what we are doing.' Does he now,' the policeman said. 'Yes, he bloody well does,' I snapped 'and he's given me permission to use the full extent of his estate and the river.' It's odd, but the name of a big landowner still pulls a lot of weight in the country particularly when he's a J.P. and local big-wig too.

"Suddenly the second policeman spoke up. 'We had a very famous bloke down here a couple of years ago,' he said. 'He was taking nude pictures. He sells them all over the world. Now, *what* was his name?…

Harry something or other. I think it was double barrelled… I can't quite remember…'

" 'Was it Harrison Marks?' I queried. 'That's it,' said the policeman. 'Well, that's me,' I said.

"The effect was electric. Suddenly both policemen beamed, they relaxed completely and grabbed my hand.

" 'Well, I'm blessed,' said the first one. 'Fancy meeting you. We've got one of your calendars in the station. I wish you'd come back and sign it.'

"Then he talked about the old boy. 'You know, there can't be more than half a dozen people a week ever use that road. It doesn't lead anywhere at all. It's a chance in a million that chap ever came down. What caused the trouble is that he's the local Methodist lay-preacher.'

"Interruptions can be amusing, though. It was by the same salmon river on a really beautiful, hot summer day, I'd climbed up a tree to get some elevation and I glanced up and there, walking down the track was a fisherman, waders, rods, hat, flies, the lot.

" 'Cover-up, girls,' I hissed, 'someone coming.' But the girls were feeling skittish and instead of grabbing their robes, they linked arms and walked down the track to meet him.

"Tony, I and the assistants dived into the bushes, but quick.

"This poor chap walked round the corner smack into five beautiful girls absolutely starkers. 'Good afternoon,' they trilled, and kept on walking. Poor chap. He stood rooted to the spot. He dropped his rod, but he just stared straight ahead. He seemed terrified to turn round. When he did pluck up the courage to look, the girls were round the corner out of sight. He pushed his hat back. Then he sat down on the hedgebank and lit a pipe which he knocked out immediately. All the time he kept looking at the corner — but he never plucked up the courage to go and look around it. After five minutes or so he moved off.

"The girls came out of the trees giggling. I said, 'If you ever do that again I'll sack you all on the spot.'

"Mind you, I didn't feel so clever when we got back to the pub where we were staying. I was having a drink at the bar when this same chap walked in. To put it mildly, there was a spot of tension. Everyone shut up at once. He glared at the landlord who, in turn, glared back. Only one man in the bar seemed unaffected, and he looked up at the fisherman.

'Hello,' he said, lad a good day? 'Yes,' he replied very tersely glaring at all the others in the bar. 'I got a nine-pounder… and it's hanging in the kitchen to prove it.' Then he swallowed his drink and marched out.

"The buzz of conversation restarted. The landlord must have seen my quizzical expression. He leant confidentially across the bar 'Got a touch of the bloody sun, that chap,' he said, 'or else he's the biggest liar in Christendom. He reckons he was walking down the river track this afternoon, and he turned a corner and ran smack bang into five beautiful girls, all in their birthday suits, absolutely starkers. Did you ever hear anything like it? Described them in detail: redhead, a blonde — a natural blonde he swears — one jet black. The bloody liar. I'm used to fishermans' stories, but that one's a bit too tall, isn't it?'

" 'You can see some funny things down by that river nowadays,' he said knowingly to the rest of the bar. Then he moved away murmuring, 'Bloody mermaids.'

Yes, location can be fun.

The locations for a sequel to "Naked" were fixed up. Next came the casting. And from that followed a salutary lesson which, at a pinch, can be paralleled to the old Naval toast, 'Here's to wives and sweethearts… and may they never meet." It happened like this:

Jill arrived at the studio about a month before the film was due to go on location. She was tall, slim and blonde and at the audition she moved like a cat. Her body undulated and her breasts, firm and taut, moved with a graceful rhythm.

Clearly, she was very attracted to Harrison Marks and so was he to her.

Almost immediately they fell in love and in no time at all they were lovers. Again, it was a swinging affair. They really matched each other and Harrison Marks thought, for the first time, "I'm going to enjoy making this film." Six weeks on location with Jill seemed like bliss.

Then, two days before the film was due on location, Susan turned up at the studio wanting to be a model. She was, Harrison Marks decided, one of the most gorgeous women he had ever been asked to photograph, and there and then he decided to use her in the film.

He told his secretary, "This girl is magnificent, and she's got to be in.

So Susan was told: "I'm going away the day after tomorrow to start work on a film. If you want six weeks' work starting then, you've got the job." She was overjoyed. The offer was so completely unexpected that all she could do was to stand there nodding her head.

So they all arrived in the West Country, Jill, Susan and thirty-five members of the cast and production team.

Fitting thirty-five people into some of the small hotels where they stayed was difficult and often people were forced to share rooms. George arranged that he would share a room with Stuart, who had been roped in to play a comedy part in the film.

The affair with Jill was to be kept secret since Harrison Marks, dealing with a dozen women at a time, didn't want any jealousy to arise or any suggestion of favouritism to upset the shooting. Alas, life with women can become complex as many a man knows.

Stuart was to find himself home base for a series of late nocturnal movements in the hotel. He did not know quite what would be happening from night to night. Sometimes he would be asked to change rooms with Jill and on other occasions George vanished for most of the night leaving him alone.

Monogamy, the cliché says, is the concept of woman: polygamy appeals much more to the man.

So it may, but most men are terrified of the results of it should ever any two separate sections of a polygamous association meet. An angry woman is hell — two angry women, no matter how much they hate each other, have a habit of ganging up on the offending male.

The situation developed like this: Susan was a gorgeous creature, but new to the film business. She was receptive and delightful, and she had to be schooled. Now, at this stage, Harrison Marks should have been warned: the tell-tale signs were all about. There was a feel of static electricity in the air when they met and talked. Naturally, in the hot-house atmosphere of filmmaking it had to spark.

There was a growing bond between them and one night Harrison Marks said, "Look, Sue, we'll have to break off the schooling for an hour while I fix up the shooting schedule with Tony. I'll pop up to your room later, and we'll finish then."

Whether one could legitimately compare Harrison Marks' follies with Tom Jones' aptitude for trouble finding is debatable. There are, in the next sequence of events, strong similarities with the Tom Jones story.

The setting, remember, was a country inn. The shooting conference finished and Harrison Marks went up to Susan's room. And there was Susan lying on the bed in an almost identical pose as Lady Bellaston in "Tom Jones" and with an expression on her face which clearly indicated that, even if she wasn't saying them, she was certainly thinking her ladyship's famous lines to Tom: "In London, it is considered impolite to keep a lady waiting."

Susan was naked; the bed clothes were turned down to her knees. The contours of her body and the fine auburn hair assumed quite a different aspect than when seen through a viewfinder. Fine flowing locks on a crisp white pillow, tenderness and affection — there were transports of delight.

Fulfilment tempered the ecstasy. "Hell," Harrison Marks thought, "what about Jill at the other end of the hotel?"

Guilt struck him doubly, from the east wing and from the west wing simultaneously. And never ever must the twain meet.

Back in his room, he said with conviction: "Stuart, we've got to plan this operation damned carefully, damned carefully." And it wasn't only the film that was on his mind.

For a week all went well, smooth and as sweet as a cream milk pudding, though not quite as sustaining. Neither girl suspected anything. Alternate evenings seemed to work well.

But the demon drink undid everything. A party in the bar, too much liquor flowing and Susan, who as it were, was on a "night off" became amorous. "Can I see you later, George, darling?" she whispered. "Sure," the unwary George agreed.

Then later, Jill murmured: "I'll leave the door, sweetheart."

Sitting on his own bed in the room with Stuart, as the drink wore off, a realisation hit him, "Stuart," he said, "I don't think you're going to see much of me; I've got a busy night ahead.

"Hell," he explains. "I was in love with both of them, but apart from that I simply couldn't afford to let either walk out on the film."

Such is martyrdom. He faced his ordeal bravely.

Drink either kills or inflames passion. Susan was exceptionally passionate that night. She was demanding, exciting and exhausting until finally, with murmured sweet nothings, she fell asleep.

No sleep for Harrison Marks, however. He daren't. He lay there frantically concentrating, saying to himself: "Stay awake, stay awake." It was like counting sheep. The effect was soporific. Nevertheless, he succeeded. Certain that Sue was sleeping, quietly, slippers in hand, he crept out of the room, down the corridor — to Jill.

"Oh, I've had the hell of a night," he complained. "We've gone through tomorrow's filming shot by shot and," he added quickly, "I've got to be up at the crack of dawn to finish the schedule off.

"I don't know what it was, probably all the fresh sea air and exercise we were getting, but that night of all nights Jill was fantastically passionate. Much later she fell asleep — but until she did I had to lie there forcing my eyes open. At last, I kissed her and whispered, 'I must get up sweetie, to see Tony.' And I crept out.

"Switchback. Down the corridor and back to Susan. I kissed her and whispered, 'I must get up darling, and go and talk to Tony.' "

The white stuff had come up outside. It was dawn, and the light streamed round the edges of drawn curtains. Birds were singing, the dawn chorus was at full crescendo. There was a blackbird outside which sounded to Harrison Marks like the old time Flying Scotsman screaming through Crewe station with its whistle going full blast.

Success demands its own particular sacrifices. One film-maker that morning felt like a sacrificial offering upon a heathen altar, a bit rough round the edges and slightly burned up.

Susan smiled, and Jill smiled. The film continued smoothly and successfully. They both went on to make big reputations — as film actresses — so in all fairness it was best to change their names. This is, of course, a book for serious students of seduction, and not in any way for Peeping Toms.

Horrible Peeping Toms. Those sick sad creatures of vicarious experience who go to extreme limits just for a look. What a plague they are to nude photographers: they arrive at the secret location as if drawn by that same magnetism which brings a homing pigeon to its roost.

Shooting the beach scenes on a secluded stretch of the Cornish coast one peeper regularly appeared, crouching low on the cliff skyline, camouflaged with netting twigs and greenery, and carrying a set of powerful binoculars. An unexpected hump would appear on the horizon — it would be him, peering intently from his disguise.

No chance to chase him away — it was far too difficult a climb up the steep cliff face and the unit could not afford one man permanently on guard duty.

Clearly, Harrison Marks reasoned, the man is a "nut". He is a psychological case, so let us try psychological treatment. It had to be done because even the most hardened model is unnerved by being spied upon. Out of the context of the location, the girls were modest as women anywhere.

"Next time this chap appears," Harrison Marks instructed the cast and crew, "don't move a muscle to let him know we've seen him. Carry on completely naturally."

The set was rigged, cameras fixed and shooting began. But one girl was positioned with her back to the cliff, round her neck a pair of the most powerful binoculars it is possible to buy.

Sure enough, Tom appeared. The filming went on without interruption and Tom grew bolder, creeping nearer and nearer to the cliff edge.

Suddenly Harrison Marks said: "Right, fix him now." The girl spun round, glasses to her eyes. Rapidly, she focussed and they met lens to lens.

The effect was quite dramatic. At a distance of a couple of hundred yards or so Tom was visibly shocked. He dropped his binoculars and looked stunned. Then he leapt to his feet and bounded away, jumping from tuft to tuft of the coarse grasses and hurling himself across the cracks and gullies.

It was remarkable. There wasn't a soul within a quarter of a mile of him, yet he appeared terrified.

He never came back.

Harrison Marks says: "I cannot stand being overlooked or snooped on… on the whole, it reminds me of another incident, not by any means as distasteful, but a little nerve-racking.

"At the time, however, I felt that I was being watched by the whole world and his wife, and they were watching me tumble from triumphant conquest to abysmal failure. Private things should be private and, above all, private failures should be very private.

The girl in the case was Eva. Eva with the unpronounceable surname and a zest for life which was unconquerable.

If life with Susan and Jill had been wearing at least the outcome was successful. In this case it was defeat — utter and total defeat; unconditional capitulation… to put it bluntly, he ended up whacked.

Everybody in London loved Eva. She had come to London after the Hungarian revolution, and she really made the city swing. In no time at all she was a "must" guest at every party. Her good looks alone would justify her inclusion. But as well, Eva was enormous, bubbling fun and George and she often went out together. Usually, they met about 11.30 in the evening and went out for a hilarious party at a restaurant or club.

"It never occurred to me why we met so late," Harrison confesses. "I just thought she worked late or something. In fact, I thought she was in television… she had a fantastic knowledge of TV. She knew every single show and all the people in them right down to the bit players.

"We always finished the night with me dropping her at her flat in Marble Arch and buzzing of home — worn out from laughing as a rule."

Then one evening at a party, Eva burst out: "George, darling, we neffer 'ave ze times to feenesh a talking proper. I sink eet es goot eff you are spending ze weekend wiz me and we see more off each other, you agree?"

"I do agree," said Harrison Marks. "We should have a ball… but I can't make it Friday," he interrupted her. "It will have to be lunchtime Saturday."

"Vunderful "she agreed.

But at nine o'clock exactly on Saturday morning the Harrison Marks' bedside phone rang.

"Hell," he says, "I hadn't got home until after four."

"Vere are you, George?" the voice yelled. "You must have bloody early lunches in Hungary," he protested.

The calls came at intervals of 25 minutes and eventually, bathed and brushed up, he made it to the Marble Arch flat soon after 11.30. He received a rapturous welcome. "My goodness me," he noted. "She lives well."

And this morning she was looking scintillating, really gorgeous. She must have been one of the most exciting and beautiful women London had seen for years.

She was dressed in a casual blouse, skin-tight pants and barefooted.

Immediately, she grabbed him. "I'd never kissed her before," he says. "And what I'd been missing… brother!

"Look," said Harrison Marks. "I've booked a table for lunch. Then I thought we could mooch around a bit and take in a theatre before dinner tonight." So he explained his plans as the drinks flowed — that is when he could get a chance to talk between the burning kisses.

Suddenly, as if she had been given an electric shock, Eva leapt up. "What's the time?" she demanded. "Twenty-to-one," said George. "Help," she screamed and belted off into the adjoining bedroom.

"A couple of seconds later I heard a man's voice; I recognised it — then music followed; she had switched on the television. 'That's a funny thing,' I thought, watching the telly while she's getting dressed.' "

Harrison Marks reflected for a few minutes and collected his thoughts and breath.

Soon a voice called "George, darling, come and help me." George went through into the bedroom… and gasped.

"Let me tell you," he says. "I never had any penchant for life behind the Iron Curtain, but if any commissar ever clapped eyes on a comrade attraction like this one, nothing at all — not the crown jewels or even freedom could ever make him defect."

Eva was naked. "The most magnificent specimen of womanhood I can ever recall seeing," says Harrison Marks. "She was a lithe, superbly modelled figure, bronzed to a deep golden tan. Only her breasts were a slightly lighter shade — she must have worn a bikini to sunbathe, but only occasionally — and, even though she was lying down, the rose-like proud hillocks were each tipped by firm protruding nipples."

"George," she sighed. "Make love to me."

"I moved to turn off the television set at the foot of the bed. 'No leave it on,' she insisted. With an elegant grace she uncoiled from the bed. That was the only way to describe it, and in a flash my shirt and the rest of my clothes were scattered on the floor.

"It was like lying with a tigress. Then she sighed and squirmed against me and murmured, 'You were magnifique, my darling.' I felt flattered… then suddenly I became aware of the strident tones of David Colman in

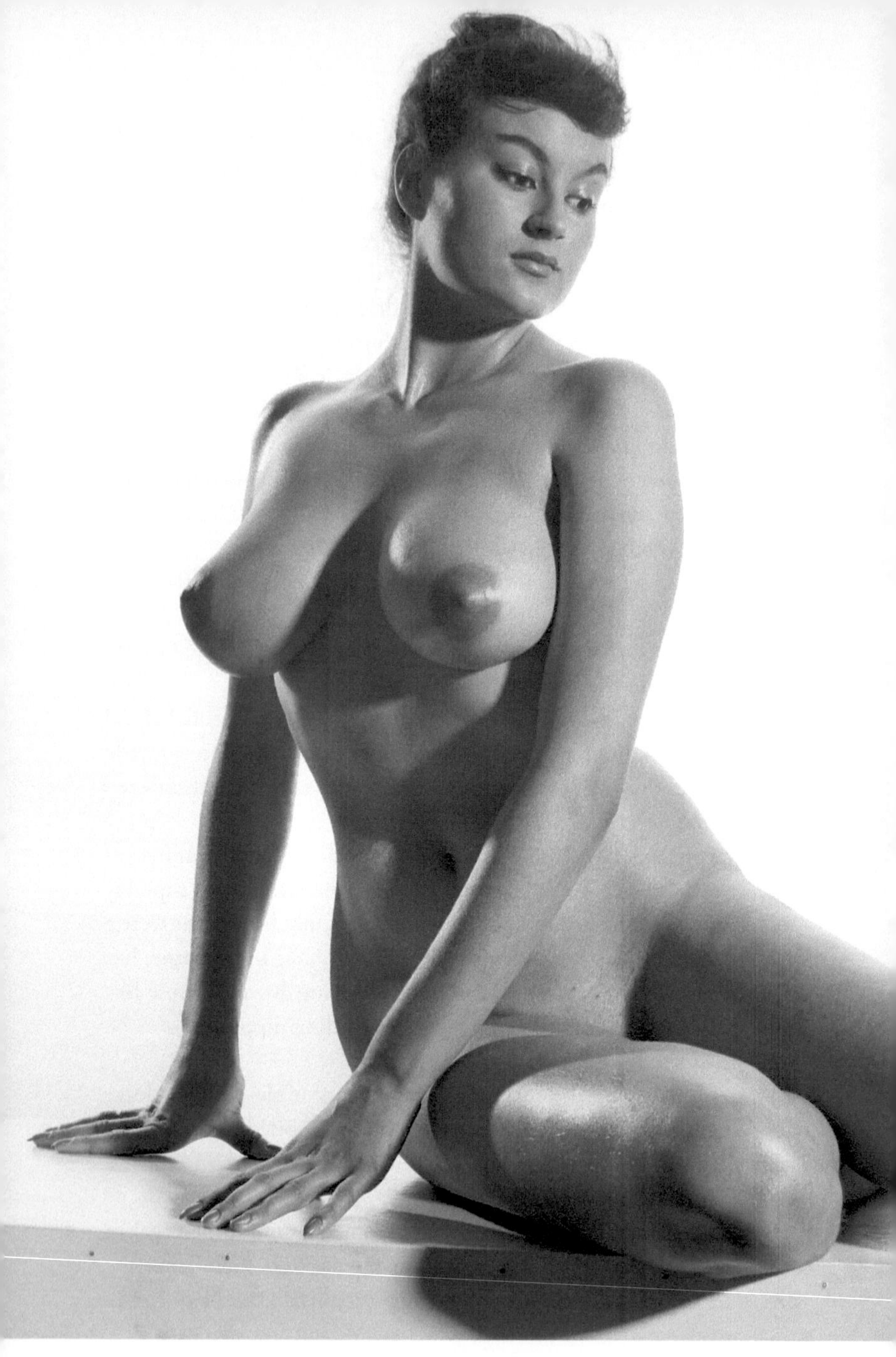

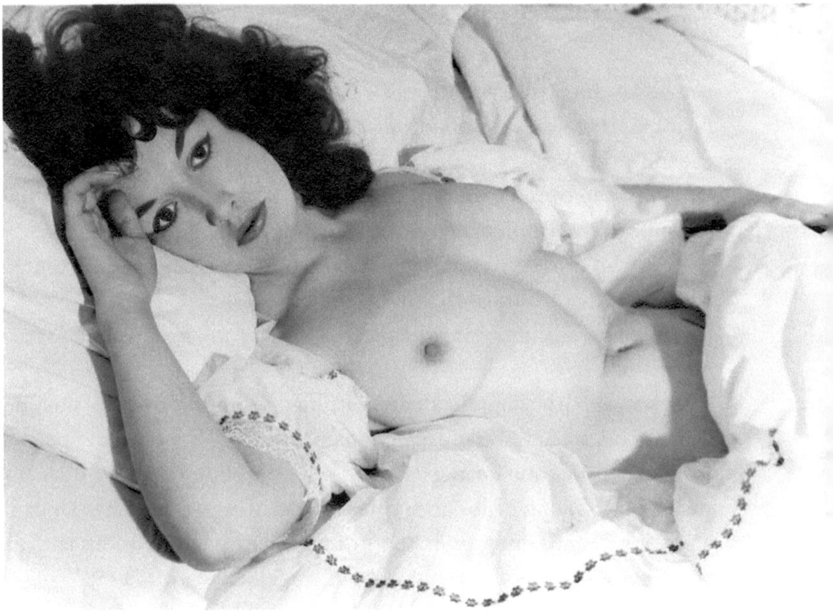

Above: The adorable Jean Sporle (Spaul), who when not modeling worked in the office in Gerrard Street

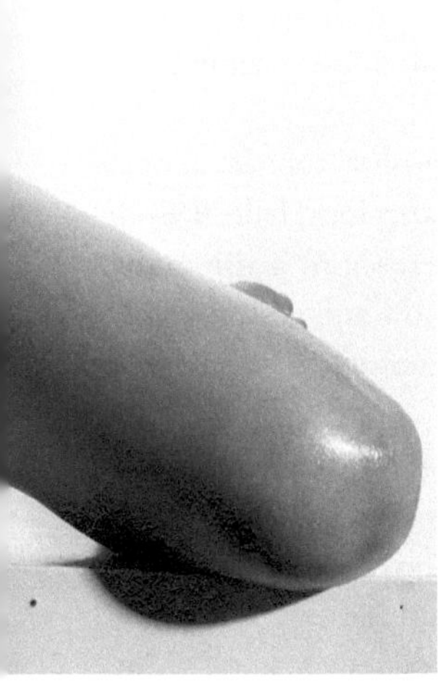

Left: Buxom Erica from Germany

my ear. And she whispered, 'Switch it to I.T.V. I love Eamonn Andrews' voice.'

"We lay silently. I was dying to say sweet nothings, but it's hard to be romantic to the roar of motocross and Murray Walker yelling above the din.

"I switched over. Vonderful; Eva sighed. 'It's John Rickman — I think he's a beautiful gentleman; such a sexy moustache.'

"It was all those ginks staring over his shoulder straight at the camera who upset me. I wanted to pull up the bedclothes.

" 'George, darling,' Eva whispered, stroking my hair. 'Make love to me again.'

"It was embarrassing; Rickman chatting up Andrews over my shoulder. But Eva became even more affectionate.

"That set the tone for the day. Rickman burbling on about such and such a horse giving 11 lbs. to another… and being a trier; Clive Graham reporting Piggott's mount under pressure; Alan Weeks with his left jabs and right crosses… and Eva saying, 'George, make love to me.'

"By the time the wrestling started I felt as if I had done three rounds with Mick McManus. I imagined myself trapped on the ropes and Eva leaning up and whispering, 'George, make love to me,' and my saying, 'What, with all the people watching?'

"It wasn't Mick McManus in the ring that day, but some equally fearsome and agile brute, and it was the first time I had ever watched a heavyweight contest and felt that I was in a similar tangle — only I was tangled up on the bed.

"The commentator's voice droned on in that hushed tone he adopts — 'Boston, double hammer head-lock, toe-lock, arm-lock, half-Nelson; Kent Walton could have been describing me. There wasn't a grip in the wrestling handbook which Eva didn't seem to know and wish to apply. That was part of the trouble; she matched her amorous moods to that of the telly programme then showing.

"Everything jumbled up. Arms, legs, breasts, hot passionate lips, voices… 'George, make love to me'… turn up; it's Dr. Who… turn it down; it's the News… 'love me, George'… hands that wash dishes… Danger Man, boom! boom! boom!… the Morecambe and Wise show — rah, rah, rah… 'George, love me'… a Guinness does you good… (by

God, I needed one)… On the Braden Beat… (he was not as beat as I was)… at last the weather — a depression filling up off Iceland… clouds will disperse but a rain belt will drift… drift… drift… drift…

"I drifted, in my own echo chamber, into deep, deep, deep oblivion. Guinness did me good, little jabbing arrows pointed at my burning throat, my back pains eased as soothing hands caressed me… God, I could use some of that cool, soothing ointment — and not just for my back… I found myself telling Wilfred Pickles how Philosan had fortified me… Hell! I could read all about myself in the *People* tomorrow… I was too tired to play football, and a tonne of Shredded Wheat couldn't have renewed my energy… and why Big Fry didn't fling all those birds off the turrets of their castle into the sea and eat the stuff himself, I couldn't understand… Women, women, women… Katie came in and placed a big bowl of man appeal on the table. Then, bang — she stripped off… oh, no, no, no, NO! NO! NO! The picture faded and rushed into itself… a receding pinpoint of light. Then blackness; blessed blackness.

"I didn't fall asleep; I passed out."

"It was two o'clock when I awoke — the first Sunday in years that I had missed a lunch-time drink in Paddy Kennedy's pub. Chirpy, chirpy, laughing Eva came in with breakfast. 'Darling,' she said, 'it's a lovely day. I've been in the park. I thought it was a shame to wake you.'

"Five minutes after I finished my coffee she switched the telly on and whispered, 'George. 'I know,' I said, 'make love to me…

"At 6.15, I put my foot down. 'No!' I said emphatically. No. Not while Meeting Point is on… or the rest of the religious programmes.' 'George,' she pleaded, quite shocked. 'They go on for an hour and a quarter.'

" 'Thank heaven,' I muttered to myself.

"I conceded defeat about Dr. Finlay time… I felt I might end up in his casebook. I don't really remember dropping off. The box was still blaring; it must have gone on right to the bitter end. Somewhere I have a recollection of the epilogue. What else happened? I can't honestly say. By this time I was as conditioned as a parlour dog; every time she whispered, 'George… as it were, I rose to the bait.

"On Monday morning, I crept out.

"My car was outside, but I hailed a taxi. I hadn't the strength to work the clutch."

A little time later, beautiful Eva married a very, very rich Texan oilman. Very rich indeed. “Now I know why those Texans eat 2 lb. steaks for breakfast,” says Harrison Marks. “And I’ll say for sure that he must have had more in his trouser pocket than just a couple of million dollars.”

CHAPTER 11

Vivienne — Love at First Sight

YES, it was high summer in Harrison Marks' life. The sun beamed from an impeccably blue sky on to the penthouse patio with its panoramic view 25 miles across London.

Nothing seemed in sight to disturb the contentment. But far down south and even farther up north two things were happening which were to change everything. Like little ruffles and whiffs of breeze which appear to soften the hottest day but really portend a tempest, they passed almost unnoticed.

The first was that an old, old friend of Annie Walker, who had just got back from Jersey, made a telephone call to George.

The second was that up in Alloa, in Scotland, a 14-year-old boy wrote a letter in answer to a mail order advertisement.

Annie, a former Harrison Marks model, runs a model agency. She had been in Jersey during the summer and the news she had was of a young girl who had been working there as a hotel receptionist. "She's great" Annie insisted. "You really must see her. I've asked her to call you. She's a London girl but she doesn't want to go back to secretarial work now she's back."

Vivienne telephoned: "Annie tells me you want to work with me. I'd like to fix a sitting."

Harrison Marks told her that he would like to take a look at her before making a definite appointment.

She said: "We are going to work when I come down aren't we?"

Again he told her he would have to look at her before making a booking.

"I'm certainly not going to waste my time coming all the way to your studio if I'm not going to be booked. If I come down there whether you want me or not I want a sitting fee."

And Harrison Marks thought: "She's got some sparkle in her this one." He knew if Annie had recommended her then she must be pretty good and he was interested to meet a girl who could be so off-hand. An appointment was arranged for a week ahead.

It was hangover day in the studio. The night before had been a sizzler; the dawn had come thumping with sledge-hammers on Harrison Marks' temple. Weights lodged on his eyelids when he tried to open them and invisible chains held him securely to his bed. It took a feat of willpower to break them and get up.

Will-power was sufficient to get him to the studio — it deserted him at the thought of work. "No calls, no callers," he told Wynne, his secretary. "I'm not in — to ANYBODY."

And this was the day Vivienne had arranged to come. It was to prove to be the day that the re-education of Harrison Marks was to begin. The acid was to creep into the sweet life.

"At 10.30 the receptionist came to my office and said, 'There's a Vivienne Warren here and she insists you arranged a sitting with her.'

" 'Not today,' I groaned. 'Do me a favour, make some excuse. Tell her I'm not here. I've got some people here and I'm tied up. Tell her anything, but get rid of her.

" 'Ask Wynne to make out a cheque for an ordinary modelling fee for her. Tell her I'll be getting in touch with her in a week's time.' "

Harrison Marks with a hangover is not the most tractable of men. In an intractable mood he can be not only obstinate but bloody-minded. Not the man for his staff to cross. The receptionist knew this well, yet she persisted. "You'd better see her, I think. She is very lovely — she's quite exceptional."

The sight of a pretty girl at the studio is hardly calculated to raise any eyebrows but something in the girl's tone made Harrison Marks take notice and say, "All right, I'll give her five minutes."

So it happened that he met Vivienne. Vivienne carries with her a compelling air of dynamism; an inner strength glows through. She is quiet, cool and exceptionally potent. Her immediate presence staggered Harrison Marks.

His hangover-dulled senses snapped to attention; his whole metabolism was charged, the girl's very presence profoundly affected him. "If anyone but I said it," he maintains, "it would sound too naive ever to be true. Now I know it was true — it was love at first sight."

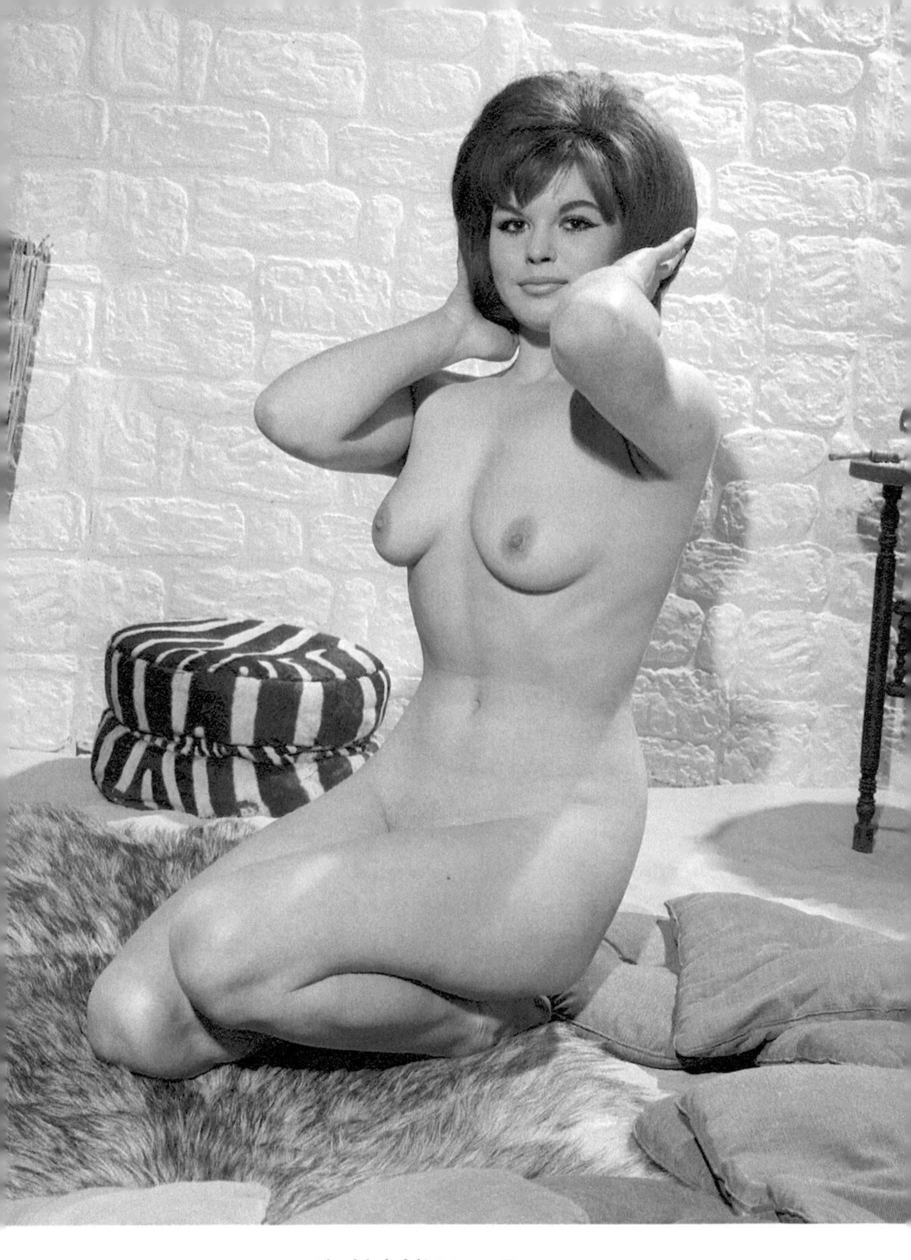

The delightful Vivienne Warren

The proof, if it is necessary, is that he married her.

"I fell in love," says Harrison Marks, "and it was a love which completely changed me, my life, the way I look at life, my relationships with people and my understanding."

It was, in all, a devastating, traumatic and searing love. A love between a man of 35 and a girl of 17 — twice her age. An impossible relationship between two incompatible, irreconcilable temperaments drawn together by a terrifying attraction.

How can a girl of 17 exert such influence? Seen from the inside, the effect could be overemphasised. But Viv exerted the same influence over nearly everyone who came in contact with her.

A woman friend, perhaps her closest, says without hesitation: "She was like a Midwich cuckoo. There was an other-world quality about her." The Midwich Cuckoos were the children of a village who were created by beings from outer space. They were beautiful but different.

So was Viv. "She was like nobody else I have ever met," Harrison Marks explains, and the affair developed quite differently from any other.

Harrison Marks continues the story: "I was knocked out by her the moment I saw her. She was wearing a brown skirt, a white blouse and a black leather jacket.

She was, in fact, one of the most beautiful women I have seen — and I've seen hundreds. My hangover forgotten, I led Vivienne into the studio.

Her figure was as good unclothed as when she was dressed. In the next hour I took dozens of shots of her.

"Draped in a fur and nothing else I thought her the most desirable creature in London. And I realised long before the sitting was over that she was a very different kettle of fish from any girl I had ever worked with.

"She was an intelligent, lively person with a very sharp mind indeed. Here was no empty-headed piece of cheesecake. It suddenly became imperative to keep her in the studio as long as possible.

"I made a date with her for dinner, determined not to let her go. And that's how it all started."

That dinner set the pattern for the weeks that followed. Vivienne was on cue the whole time, knowing every step well before George got to it, and she had the ability to sidetrack and turn the conversation any way she wanted it to go.

There was certainly no suggestion of seduction on that first night. Not, in fact, until much later.

Strangely, for all her good looks and figure, Vivienne was not a very good model. She simply had no time for it. To her it wasn't a business, it wasn't a profession. She didn't like it at all and that was it.

Vivienne's arrival posed a delicate problem. Harrison Marks was involved with another of his models. And for once it had gone beyond the stage of a casual love affair.

The girl was someone he had known for nearly five years. The affair had developed gradually and because of this was stronger than the usual "one-night stand" flirtations.

It was getting too serious to be comfortable. She was very beautiful and he was unwilling to let her go. He did not want to marry again, but the whole business was drifting unpleasantly for him — towards just that.

Then Vivienne erupted into his life. "It was a terrible mix-up. I was knocked out by Viv, but I didn't want to lose the other one. I had no way of knowing just how far things would develop with Vivienne and I'd already resigned myself to a more or less permanent relationship with the other.

"It was Viv in her very straightforward way who brought up the matter. 'You'll have to choose, George,' she said. 'Do you want her or do you want me?'

"Really, there wasn't a choice at all. I was infatuated. I had to have Viv.

"We dug each other as people. But we were complete opposites."

There wasn't one thing out of bed which she liked that he liked. It was strange that they could be so close as people and yet so opposed in so many ways.

"I battled every way I knew how not to ask her to marry me. I knew that marriage just wasn't for me. I had proved this twice already. Yet she loved me and I loved her to such an extent that my common sense was over-ruled.

At the same time I was trying to dismiss her love for me; trying to find reasons why she should want me and want to marry me without really loving me.

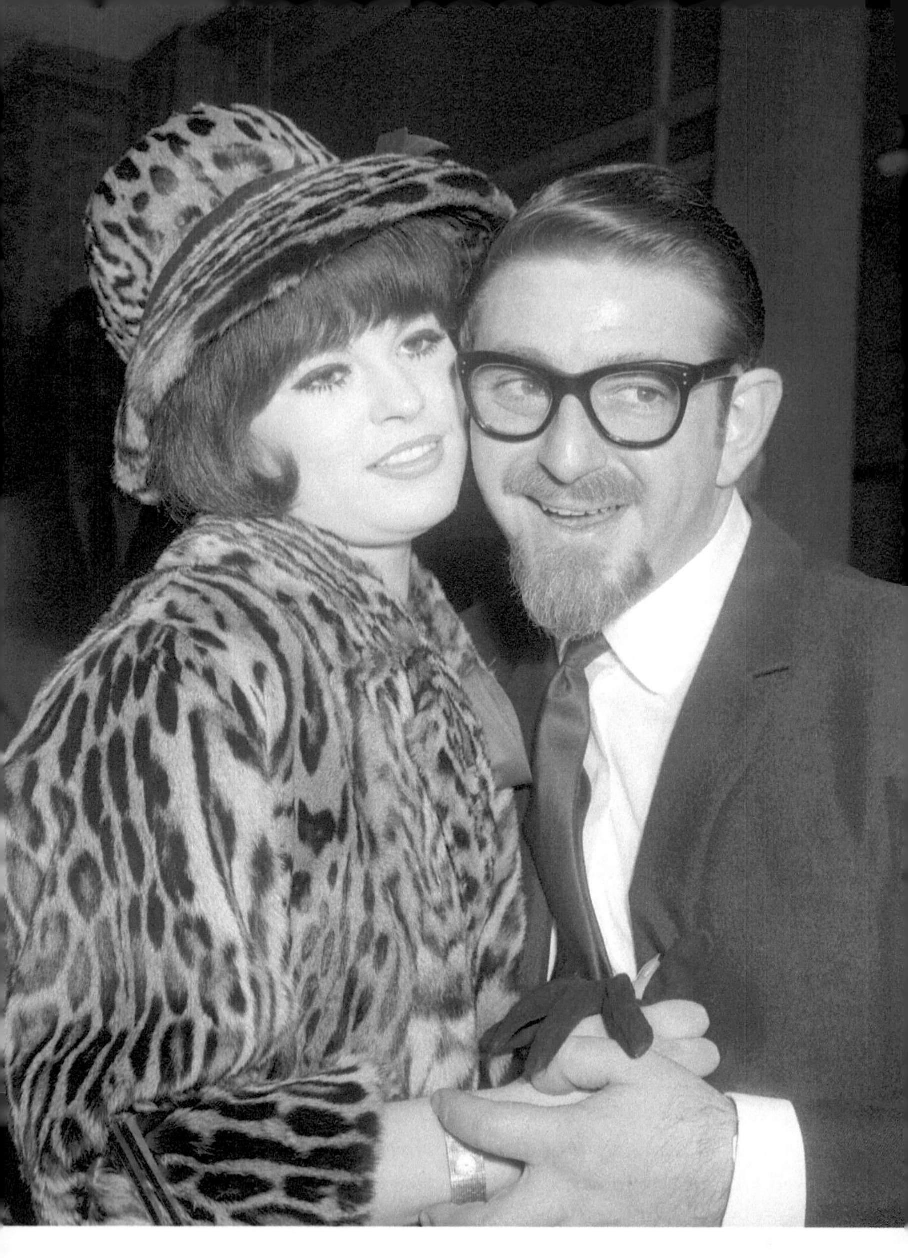

George Harrison Marks with Vivienne Warren, at Caxton Hall after their marriage on 30 November 1963

This has always been one of my big problems. I meet girls and I weigh them up and I think, 'What do they want?' It's not as though I walk around in a black cloak. They know who I am. They know I'm worth a few thousand.

"So I sum it up and most of them I don't care less about.

"Then suddenly something deeper comes along and I start to wonder. That's how it was with Viv. I suppose I should have accepted my first impressions. But I always look for something behind a girl's actions and I asked myself then, 'Is there a motive for what she's doing? Is there an angle I haven't spotted?'

"It is so easy to ruin a relationship like this and this was the main cause of the marriage collapsing — for the stupid reason that I couldn't believe my own luck. I had a girl like this, and I was still looking for faults.

" 'Where is it?' I thought. 'Where's the crack in the plaster?' Eventually I killed it all stone dead.

"I never actually popped the question. It was just accepted one day that we were going to get married and a date was set in November, 1964."

They did not live together before their marriage. If people live together and get used to it then they don't ever marry, he believes.

"I've led what people might call an immoral life. I regard it as just a free life. But I still have a tremendous regard for marriage. I believe that if you are going to marry someone then you must wait until after the ceremony before setting up as man and wife.

"Viv was my constant companion. But she had her own flat in Bryanston Square, near Marble Arch, and her own front door. And that's where she lived. She paid her own way and was completely independent.

"When I went to Caxton Hall to marry Viv I asked my second wife, Pam, along to the ceremony.

Crazy? Well, not really, for although my marriage to Pam had long since been over, we were still fond friends and when Viv and I had been mulling over the guest list it was perfectly natural, we thought, that Pam should be invited.

"But what I most definitely did not expect when I arrived that cold November morning was to find my first wife waiting to greet me on the steps.

"We hadn't seen each other for a good ten years and at first, I could hardly believe my eyes. I am now pretty sure that some smart newspaperman had raked her up from somewhere in order to get a good human interest story, but it was highly embarrassing to me.

"After all, what can you say to someone with whom marriage had been proved a disaster when you are on your way to marry someone else, especially when that someone is only 17 and young enough to be the daughter of the first marriage?

"Nothing, of course. I simply made some friendly remark and she wished me luck and I fled inside. I did not wish her any ill feeling — nor do I now — but I hoped like hell she would be gone when I got outside again after the ceremony with my bride of two minutes.

"But when I walked out with Viv on to the steps for the news cameramen to get their pictures, there she was. And it was then I noticed one of the newsmen waving her to get into the wedding group. If the rest of Fleet Street found me a little uncooperative that morning, I apologise, but I hope they now understand. At any rate, when wife number one hove in sight, I hustled wife number three back inside where wife number two and the other guests were assembled and I think I avoided being pictured with the old and the new, as it were, together. Still, that's show business."

Their honeymoon in Paris was the first George had had in three marriages. When they returned to London, for a time it looked as though they were going to make a go of it.

George was very keen to start a family. He wanted children but he had already determined that Vivienne wanted to wait a few years.

One of the reasons why the marriage with Pam did not last was that she did not want children. Time was creeping by and George did not want to wait too long.

But Vivienne had planned exactly what she wanted. She was young and wanted three or four years of marriage before having children. Harrison Marks knew that it was pointless trying to hustle her into it.

For five months they were ecstatically happy. Then the trouble started. And this is Harrison Marks' view of it: "I was an impossible bastard. I had very definite views and could not see the point of view of anyone else, including my wife.

"People directly involved with me had to take my line or lump it. Viv was by this time 18 and, naturally enough, she rebelled."

All the combustible ingredients were there for an enormous explosion. It was to come, but a little later. Looking back, Harrison Marks says: "Viv has a complete and utter honesty toward life. She will turn her back on whatever she thinks isn't right. She will walk away from what she considers wrong — irrespective of what she will lose by it.

"She taught me tolerance, regard for others' opinions and feelings. She taught me everything that is the basis for intelligent living — and this, a girl of seventeen."

Vivienne had been brought up in an orphanage. She knew next to nothing of domesticity and certainly less of the high living customary in the Harrison Marks household.

Peremptorily she announced: "I'll learn to cook," and she went to Harrods to buy some books.

She arrived back with a stack; the bill came to 27.

Harrison Marks thundered: "Cookery books £27…"

She cut him off: "If you want good cooking — there's a lot to learn."

Methodically the went through them all, page by page. In less than six months she was a fabulous cook. She would cope with a dinner party for six perfectly; no one would even notice that she had left the room to prepare the next dish. Soon she became a fine hostess, adapting to her environment perfectly… faultless makeup, hair and clothes.

And with it all, a remarkable down-to-earth common sense. But she was not, decidedly not, malleable.

Audrey Macdonald, another close friend, says: She is distinctly a girl of her times — cool and with it, but analytical."

She was young but had the sense and judgement of women twice her age.

"I couldn't realise my luck at the time. I thought only that here was an 18-year-old girl who had fallen right on her feet. I loved her and thought that as long as I gave her everything I wanted to, then she would just be there. She didn't have to think. The point is that she did think.

"She didn't consider herself a decoration for my arm. 'I am an individual and a person,' she said. 'I have my own ideas and my own attitude to life. I have my own feelings and they are not the same as yours.' This was her attitude.

"It used to get my back up and I was very indignant. I used to say 'Who the hell do you think you are?' And the battles started. But there was still this tremendous attraction. It lasted for six months. She just walked out saying that she couldn't put up with my dictatorial attitude any longer.

"We were still living in Hampstead. That was one of the things to which she had objected. She felt uncomfortable in the place. It wasn't her home but a home that someone else had created. And there were the ghosts of dozens of mistresses to remind her that she wasn't the first woman to sleep with me there.

"She had married someone who had gone through it all three times. But she was a young woman and this was her first marriage and because of it, she wanted to create her own home.

"The friends to whom she had gone got in touch with me and said, 'For goodness sake why don't you get together again. She's miserable; you're miserable.'

"Above all, I didn't take her leaving me all that seriously. I still thought that she was out to get something from me and thought 'OK, leave her be and she'll come running.'

"Eventually she did come back. But it wasn't cap in hand. She rang me up one day and said, 'What's going to happen? This is stupid.'

"We went for dinner and we were knocked out by each other again. But we didn't spend the night together. She said beforehand: 'Because I'm going out with you for dinner doesn't mean to say you can go to bed with me tonight. I want a marriage — not an affair.

"Two days later she moved back in. I started to see reason at last and promised that we would look for another home."

It was a tense situation. A few months only married, desperately in love but incompatible; trying, hoping beyond hope to find a solution to the problem. Nerves were stretched to breaking point at a time of stress and unhappiness.

Then the bombshell dropped from quite another direction. Two policemen called and informed Harrison Marks that he was to be charged because they claimed he had issued obscene films. The letter the 14-year-old boy in Alloa had written months before had come home to roost.

The shock was inestimable. In the first place, the charges were serious. If they were proved it could mean a term of imprisonment. And it would also mean the total collapse of the business… utter ruin. The most worrying aspect was that not only was he fighting the police but also an inbuilt prejudice and hypocritical attitude by certain official bodies and some sections of the public. Any police charge is a shock, even for a minor motoring offence — serious charges such as these were can be stupifying, no matter how innocent you know you are.

It all happened because of a stupid, but unavoidable, accident. For years Harrison Marks had been making short glamour films for the home movie market, thousands were on distribution through most of the reputable wholesalers.

The young boy in Alloa had answered a mail order advertisement by Nathan and Martin Lee. It was for general films. By error two of Harrison Marks' glamour pamphlets had been sent to him. His father had found them and complained to the local police who, in turn, passed the complaint to London.

The London police raided the Lees' warehouse and seized 358 films. The police had called at the studio and told Harrison Marks they might need him as a witness if they proceeded against the Lees. He couldn't quite see what evidence he could give against one of his best customers but obviously, he had to co-operate. The police worry, then, seemed to be that so-called "obscene" literature had been sent through the post.

Ten months elapsed from this visit. Then the police called again and charged him with counselling and procuring the publication of four films said by the police to be obscene.

Troubles came not singly and shock piled upon shock. "It was more than my business was worth to have that sort of smear on my name. Right away I shot round to my solicitor and asked his advice.

"I was staggered when he advised me to plead guilty, pay a fine and forget it.

" 'You must be joking,' I said. 'Plead guilty to what? There is nothing obscene in those films and I'm damned if I'm going to take this lying down. Get me the best counsel in town. We re going to fight." So, against his solicitor's advice, he defended — vigorously.

Mr. James Burge was engaged and the battle was a win, but nothing can erase the humiliation of the actual proceedings. Being locked in the cell with every known kind of felon, the climbing the stairs into the court… "prisoner in the dock"… doubts and fears are overwhelming.

The trial started and counsel for the Director of Public Prosecutions told the court that although the films were marked "Adults Only" he was submitting that in practice this was an invitation to adolescents to falsify their ages to get the films.

Harrison Marks and the Lees denied this.

The policeman was called and Burge asked how long it had taken to bring the case: "Ten months."

How long did each film last? "Four minutes."

Embarrassed, the policeman admitted that personally he didn't consider the films obscene or pornographic.

Then, incredibly, counsel for the Director of Public Prosecutions confessed that he had not seen the very films he was telling the jury were filthy, obscene and corrupting.

"And that's how we came to show them to the judge. He wouldn't hear of letting the case be tried without everyone knowing what they were trying to pass judgement on, so a projector was rigged in a back room and we all sat through a most unlikely showing — the judge, a12-man jury, counsel and me.

"From then on it was perfectly clear that the judge regarded the police case as fatuous — which it was. When it came to his summing up he told the jury to bear in mind that this was all happening in 1964, not 1864, and that what might once have been regarded as beyond the pale was now an acceptable part of modern life. They were asked to discount their own prejudices, if any, against seeing the naked female body and to judge the case solely on the issue involved: that of obscenity.

"The Lees and I were cleared completely — not guilty on any count."

So justice is done. Or is it? No account is ever taken of the weeks of devastating, distracting worry preceding such a trial. Nor of the humiliation. Nor of the fact that, in ignorant minds, some mud sticks. The fact of having stood trial is, in itself, to some people, a condemnation.

Certainly, Harrison Marks was awarded £100 costs. The case cost him more than £2,000 to defend.

Some of the police thinking on the matter is baffling. Harrison Marks tried from the very start to be helpful: "Of course, it should never ever have happened that this boy received pamphlets with nude pictures. But the Lees had no way of knowing it was a boy of 14 they were dealing with. When the police came to see me they asked a lot of questions about the films and I answered them all. I invited them to take a look at any of the 50-odd films I had in store to see if they thought there was anything indecent in any of them, but they declined. No one was complaining about the films, they said, only the fact that pictures of nudes had been sent through the mail to a juvenile. And that was someone else's concern."

It took nearly a year to come to a decision to prosecute. Perhaps, like beauty, purity is in the eye of the beholder.

During the whole of the case, Viv behaved exactly as one would expect. She never wavered. She could subjugate her own interests to loyalty at any time.

But still, the combustible situation was there: two diametrically opposed characters attempting to live in unison. Tinder and flint and whenever they touched they sparked. The smell of scorching permeated their lives. Rows, rows, rows and bitter disagreements.

She coped as well as she could but always the tremendous rows day after day, until it reached the point where both were on the edge of nervous breakdowns.

Came the day when she said finally: "I can't cope with it anymore. I love you very much, but I just can't live with you. You are just impossible to live with. And that is it."

She left. "As far as she was concerned there was no future in it for either of us.

"Suddenly I realised what an utter fool I had been. Only after she'd gone, for the second and final time, did I realise how much I needed her. But it was too late. She had gone for good, and it was all over."

It finished, but it never really ended. For Harrison Marks, that is. Viv is as much with him every minute of the day as ever she was when they lived together.

A Midwich cuckoo, they said, and not at all unkindly. She planted a cuckoo's egg in Harrison Marks' mind and still it is growing to dominate all his thoughts.

The rich man; the poor girl — who had the most to give? It is a good question.

Crack-up — and the cup of happiness shattered. And the cream in the other cups turned sour. At the studio Wynne suffered, as Harrison Marks explains:

"She would come in and say 'I've got so and so out there; he wants to spend £3,000.' I'd reply, 'Tell him to get lost.' I didn't want to know anything about anything.

"Wynne coped with that situation and the business for six months.

"Impulsively I did the most stupid things. One day while driving to the studio I decided to get out of the country — there and then. At the office I told Wynne to book a place on the car ferry that afternoon. Two hours later I was on my way to Dover. I didn't even know where I wanted to go. Poor Wynne nearly went berserk, trying to cope with me and the business. I just didn't want to know anything about what was going on.

"On the Continent I drove straight to Luxembourg where I decided I didn't want the car anymore. So I left it and caught a plane to Rome. I booked into an hotel, thought, 'What the hell am I doing here?' and checked out an hour later. So to Naples and them to Capri. There I had the only affair of my Grand Tour. It was a blazing affair with the owner of a small boutique. She was French and ran this boutique on the main avenue. I was there for about two weeks and spent the time in bed, almost non-stop.

"Then I thought, 'What am I doing here? I love a girl in England.' With that I went back to Rome. Two days later I was in Venice. I wandered about Europe like a nomad for more than two months. Every night I would go out and get raving stoned out of my head.

"At home nobody knew where I was. I would phone Wynne every other day mainly to save her sanity. I never told her where I was. After two months I had blown a thousand quid, which is not a lot till you consider most of it was spent on booze. I was back in Venice with an overwhelming desire to get back to England straight away. I caught a plane to Luxembourg, picked up the car and drove like a madman to Ostend to catch the night car ferry back to England.

"I knew that I was killing myself drinking but I couldn't care less. My liver went up the wall, but I didn't mind. Even friends telling me that

I was rapidly drinking myself into the grave didn't affect me. Only one good thing came out of this period: I devised the plot for 'The Naked World of Harrison Marks'. And it was making the film that saved me.

"I wrote, directed and produced the picture and played seven different parts. I worked solidly 18 hours a day for nearly five months. I soaked myself in it and lived for nothing else. And eventually it brought me out of my depression. The money side of it wasn't important. I have a lot of money but I don't consider it all that important.

"This is one of the things that Viv taught me b walking out. She had suddenly turned her back on everything I had to offer and this was the crippling thing for me.

Suddenly I realised that for this girl there wasn't any angle. She didn't want my money or my name. She simply loved me and I had been too blindto realise it.

"Since leaving me Viv has never asked me for a penny. She took only one thing when she left — a painting. It was one that I had bought her in the South of France while we were on holiday.

"I had bought an original Salvador Dali and there was a Jean Cocteau — which she fell in love with. It was a profile — very simple, very beautiful.

"When she left she said, 'There's only one thing I want — my painting.' She said it was a reminder of the very happiest time of our marriage. And that's all she wanted. Nothing else."

CHAPTER 12

Naked as Nature Intended

THE film "Naked as Nature Intended" opened at the Cameo Moulin, in Windmill Street, in the heart of the West End of London. There had been little or no advance publicity even though the premiere was in all senses a "first" — the first all-British nudist film, the first full-length feature to be produced by Harrison Marks and the first feature to be shown at the cinema since it had changed from being a cartoon and news cinema.

From the opening night it was a sensation. When Harrison Marks arrived at the cinema there were queues along both pavements, one stretching down to Shaftesbury Avenue. It was so novel that the magazine *Film Renter* published a full page picture of the queues, astonished at the enormous public interest in a "nudie" film.

Again it happened with Harrison Marks' third feature picture. Running flashing lights emphasised it. From morning to late night they flashed, bright and garish flash… flash… flash… all day, every day.

And inside, at the booking office, the ticket machine went click… click… click… all day as the cash tinkled into the till. For the second time in Harrison Marks' life — BONANZA!

"The Naked World of Harrison Marks" success!

But, does any man ever feel more naked than when standing in front of his bank manager?

If anything, his bank manager knows more about him than even his doctor.

For months the queues gathered daily at the cinema door. And this in spite of the fact that only one critic had reviewed the film.

"They came because my name is so well established in this field — and for no other reason," Harrison Marks concluded.

Who was the odd critic out? The only write-up the film got, and a good one, was in the *Jewish Chronicle.*

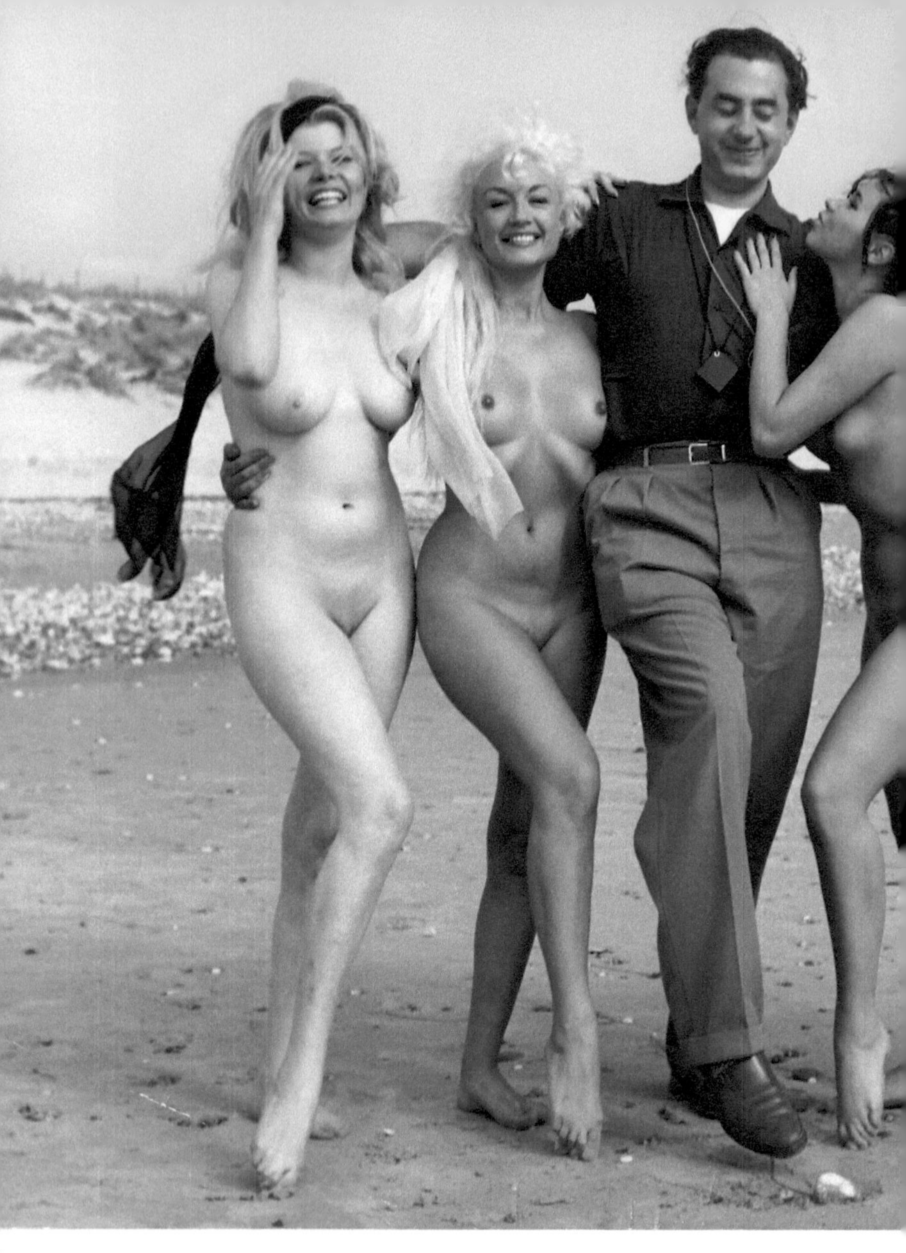

Left to right: Bridget Leonard, Pamela Green, Roy Pointer, Jackie Salt, Angela Jones and Petrina Forsyth, during a break from the filming of 'Naked as Nature Intended'.

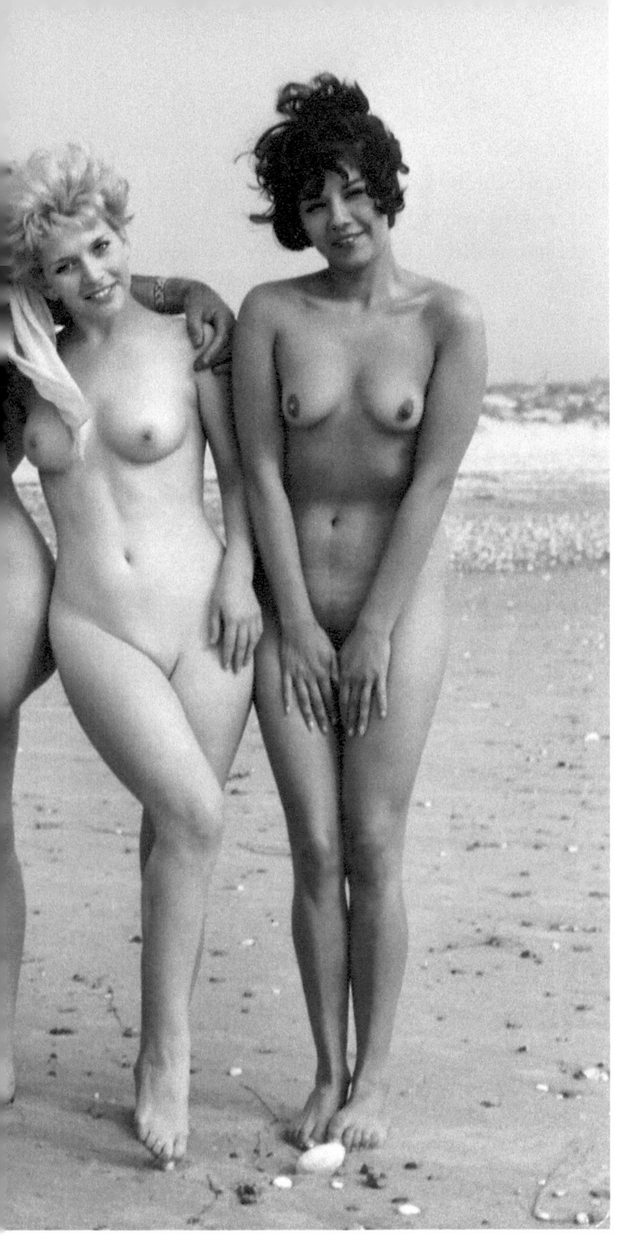

The cash was rolling in and Harrison Marks was free and untrammelled, no wife, no worries, the world was his oyster and the days of wine and roses were on in a big way.

There was the flat in Hampstead leased for £9,000, the finest of cars, the best food that money could ever buy. And there were girls — the loveliest girls London and the world could provide.

Nightly, the big maroon Rolls ferried its cargo of delight to the penthouse near the Heath. Wine and roses and again the sweet, sweet smell of tender success. But at what cost?

Harrison Marks is reluctant to say. But the account books show quite clearly that the flat and day-to-day living expenses come to £200 a week. "I live fairly modestly," he explains. "If I wanted to splash out, I could. But I don't really like flashy extravagance." Modest? 200 a week?

In all fairness, yes; it is modest. Any building society, considering an application for a mortgage will work on one-fifth of a man's income to decide what he can afford to pay.

Harrison Marks' talents had by this time brought him a huge income from the film, from the home movie business he had pioneered, from the magazine and books and from the studio. He had worked for it — and really worked.

"Apart from this," he details, "I was making between £ 1,000 and £ 1,500 a week from side deals I had set up. If I made less than £ 1,000, I had a niggling feeling I was going broke.

"I really don't like talking about this type of money," he says defensively. "I know what it's like to live on less than £15 a week, and it seems boastful."

Surely, the answer is that any man can start where Harrison Marks did — borrow the cash to buy a second-hand camera and if he has the talent, end up ten years later living at the modest rate of £200 a week.

(Author's note: Incidentally Harrison Marks is setting up a shop in Gerrard Street to sell cameras and photographic equipment… the rich get rich and the poor get — credit.)

"If I am an incurable romantic," Harrison Marks confesses, "about this time there happened the most romantic episode in my life. I had gone to Paris to see a very, very famous fashion model and the whole thing was ridiculous.

She didn't speak a word of English and I didn't speak of syllable of French, yet we fell violently in love.

"The first night I took her out. I arrived at her flat with a pencil and a drawing pad and we communicated by pictures. I'd meant to be in Paris for three days but after that I stayed for three weeks, and we were never out of each other's sight. Goodness, we were in love! It was love and romance and Paris all mixed up together. We would wander all round the city hand in hand. She was really big over there and in constant demand but she just turned down all the jobs to be with me.

"We simply couldn't bear to be apart. It got to the stage when I decided to pack it all up in London and start afresh in Paris.

"But there were so many snags, that proved impossible. Then she wanted to quit Paris and come to London. It was only when I did get back to London that I managed to collect my senses and reason that whichever way it went it would be impossible and unfair on one or the other of us. But it still kept on; as fast as I could I was back in Paris. When we were apart we wrote long, passionate letters — and we had to take them to friends to be translated.

"It's difficult to keep love alive with a permanent chaperone, in the form of a translator, there. So it had to be 'Au revoir'. But I still keep a copy of *Elle* with her on the cover... my silent cherie."

Love does not, unfortunately, immunise one from colds... and Harrison Marks caught a cold. It was thick and heavy and getting worse. He felt awful when Margo telephoned. 'No, darling,' he apologised, 'I can't possibly see you tonight, I feel deadly. I'm going to have dinner with Gerry and Patrina and go straight to bed.' "

Gerry Lorden, the songwriter who wrote The Shadows' hits among many other things, was his next door neighbour, and his wife Patrina was one of Harrison Marks' former models.

Round at the Lordens' flat four places were set for dinner. "Who else is coming?" Harrison Marks asked.

"Well, Margo is; she rang and said you'd asked her to call and see if it would be all right for her to come, too."

"The little bitch," said Harrison Marks. "But I'll tell you one thing, Gerry, she's not — definitely not — staying with me tonight."

Margo had different ideas. After dinner, back in George's flat, before he had time to ring for a taxi, she started to undress. "Darling," he said, "you've got to go home. I'm too ill."

Poor chap, he was too ill to argue.

Somehow Margo had failed to learn to differentiate between a soothing clinical touch and the hot hands of desire. She was determined to soothe, all she did was excite.

Poor, poor chap — and him with a temperature! By morning he had raging pneumonia. And it wasn't until six weeks later that he got out of bed.

Then he did an idiotic thing. Before he was really better, he rushed up to Manchester to make a personal appearance when the film opened there. For his trouble he was rushed back 184 miles flat out in the back of an ambulance.

Bed again and another burden for Mrs. Dolly Lowe, his housekeeper for 14 years. She is, he declares: "One of the four people who keep me living — Dolly, Wynne, Toni and Tony."

"Dolly," he assures everybody, "rises above everything. In her eyes I can do no wrong; she is the most forgiving of mother-characters.

"She has caught the back-lash of my love affairs and had to comfort more heartbroken girls than I care to recall. She tells them all, 'don't try to chain him or he'll rebel. He is so wrapped up in his work that he cannot stand to be chained.' And that's perfectly true, and that's why so many love affairs have gone wrong — they tried to chain me and change me. It wouldn't work."

So Harrison Marks was on his back again, drugged to the eyeballs, too ill to care. The doctor was calling three times daily and diplomatic Dolly had to manipulate the string of callers so that no two girlfriends arrived at the same time. With the skill and acumen of a signalman at Clapham Junction, she manipulated the times of arrival and departure to the minute — four minutes clear between one leaving and one arriving. Alas, one day she went out to do the shopping and the system collapsed.

Three girls arrived simultaneously and the girl who was on "bedside sympathy" duty at the time, let them in. Dolly came back to find all four round the bed giving loving looks to George and looking daggers at each other.

Gerry Lorden made his daily call and walked into the bedroom. He stopped in his tracks. "Christ! "he said. "Get the doctor; he's going — I always knew it would be like this the day he died. George on his deathbed surrounded by beautiful, weeping women."

He didn't die. There was too much wine left in the jug and too many roses to be picked.

"Gerry Lorden always said it would be my greatest exit line," says Harrison Marks. "I'm glad I missed it."

CHAPTER 13

Model Cats

"I ALMOST forgot to tell you about my cats. I adore them and I am almost as famous for my cat photography as for my women. I was asked to illustrate Sir Compton Mackenzie's book of cats. An honour, and when the book came out I was gratified at the wide praise for the pictures. Cats are less troublesome than women.

"I publish a cat calendar as well as the pin-up one. One year a bishop, no less, wrote for one and another of those embarrassing postal mix-ups happened. Instead of getting his cats he received the pin-ups. Fortunately, this time, there were no dire consequences. His Lordship wrote me a pleasant letter saying that really he would prefer the 'other kind of feline'. We sent it to him immediately… but he didn't return the nudes.

"I've had one other flirtation with the church after I had finished shooting "Naked as Nature Intended".

"A man called at the studio and said he had met me while the film unit was working on the Bedruthal Steps — a location in Cornwall.

"Of course, I didn't remember him, but I pretended to and he seemed very happy. 'I've got the most beautiful wife, as you probably remember,' he said. 'I think she would make a wonderful model and I'd love you to take some pictures of her as I admire your work so much. Will you photograph her in the nude?'

"I told him that this was very flattering, but that I did not undertake private commissions. All my work was for publication.

"If I could only see her, he burbled on, I would be sure to want to photograph her.

"They lived miles away and thinking that she would never come to London just on the off-chance of being photographed, I told him, 'Send her up some time and I'll take a look at her.' Three weeks later the girl arrived out of the blue. She was certainly attractive, 22 — and keen to start work.

" 'Well, first of all, I'd better take a look at your figure,' I told her.

"She was rather shy at first. Then she said, 'My husband wants you to take these pictures of me in the nude, so I suppose now I'm here I'd better undress.'

"I waited as she undressed in the dressing room. "Blushing slightly, she stood, hands on hips, before me.

" 'You've got a very good figure; I think I can use you.'

" 'What are you going to do with the pictures after you've taken them?' she asked.

"I told her I thought her husband had understood that I only took pictures for publication. 'I pay the model and then use the photographs for my calendars and magazine.'

"That could be a little awkward,' she said. 'Because of my husband's work, you know. People might talk.'

"I thought what the hell has her husband's work got to do with it.

" 'What does he do for a living, then?' I asked.

" 'Don't you know?'

" 'No'.

" 'He's a vicar.' "

There was even an admiral's wife. The Naval officer was in his fifties and thought his wife, a woman of 32, was the most beautiful thing in the world. He had seen Harrison Marks' work and asked him to photograph his wife in the nude.

The photograph, measuring three feet by four feet, now hangs above the Admiral's bunk in his cabin… the old seadog!

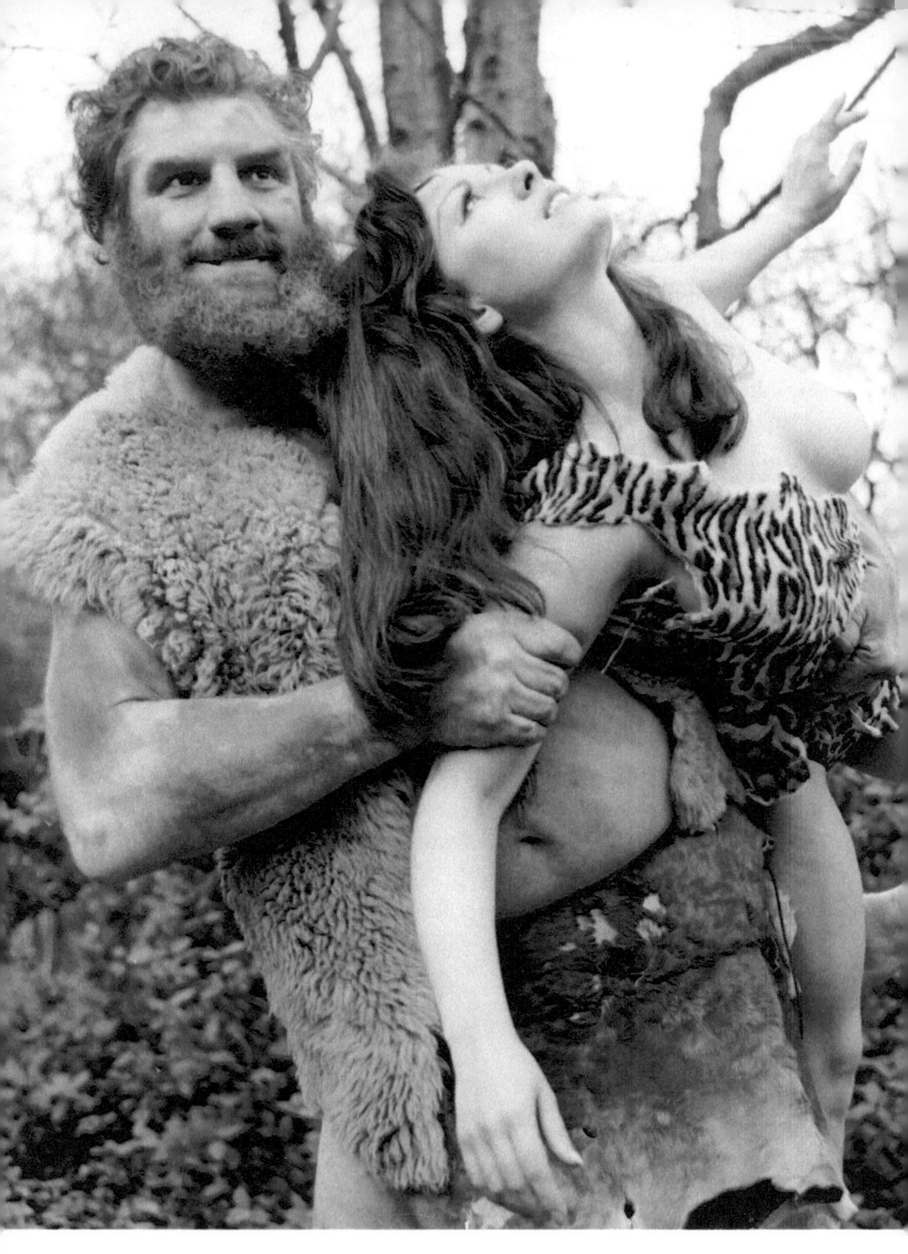

Bruno Elrington and June Palmer on the set of the film, 'The Nine Ages of Nakedness' — from the Stone Age to the Topless Computer Age. Photo by Peter B. Fairbrass.

CHAPTER 14

Life Begins at Forty

Sum up the situation in two clichés: Only the good die young — and life begins at 40.

There is an end to this story… or is there? "Yes," Harrison Marks insists. "Definitely yes. I am a changed man, a fundamentally changed man. All that old stuff is over, all the rave-ups and wild marriages — it's all done with."

And the studio staff smile a wry smile which implies: "He's at his most lethal when he's settling down."

Stuart Samuel's face twitches and one can hear him thinking, "Get out the portrait of Dorian Gray."

Harrison Marks is quick to qualify his statement. "It doesn't mean I'm going to become a monk and it doesn't necessarily mean I'm giving up all the girls. Let's see how the cookie crumbles, but I'm not going to chase after it like it was going out of fashion.

"This year, 1967, I have reached a crossroads, and now I know the road I am going to take.

"The facts are simple. Vivienne changed me. She changed my life, my outlook on life, my attitude to life and people, and when all that changed my attitude to my work changed. It's only natural my work is my life.

"Now I want to see some meaning in my work. I don't mean sombre arty films or anything like that. But I have only one more nudie to finish; then I am going into feature films. So, in future — say a couple of years from now — don't pay your five bobs and expect to see only a nudie just because my name is on it.

" 'The Naked World of Harrison Marks' has been as big a success as 'Naked as Nature Intended' — in fact, it will probably make me more money. It has shown, or is showing, all round the world — even in Japan. I have spent months planning a third, The Seven Ages of Nakedness'. A lot of work has gone into it and a lot of money, but it will definitely be my last.

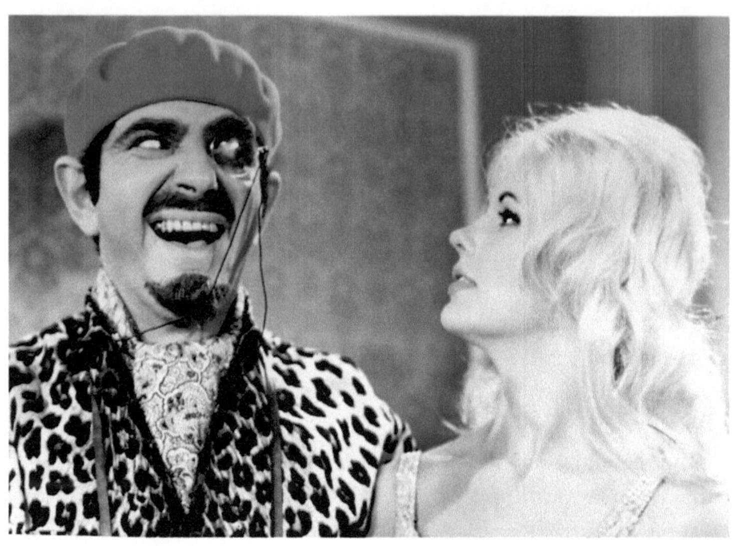

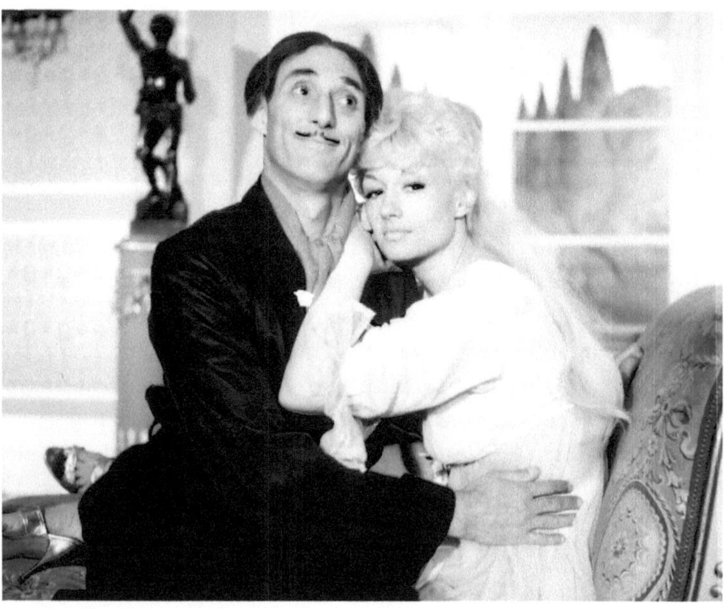

On the set of ,The Naked World of Harrison Marks' during the filming of the fictious 'Casanova Strikes Again'. Top: The Director (George Harrison Marks) and his assistant Annette Johnson. Above: Sir Aubrey Sludge (Stuart Samuels) as Casanova and Pamela Green

"Things happen to me. When 'The Naked World of Harrison Marks' was running, Bob Hartford-Davis, the man who made the last Norman Wisdom hit and dozens of others, including The Yellow Teddy Bear', saw it and liked it. Now we are joining together to make a full-length feature film in Hollywood. As well as co-producing, I will be acting in it. That's the next challenge."

("Hollywood, and all that temptation," Stuart Samuels thinks, "the picture of Dorian Gray is in for a rough old time!")

Has Harrison Marks changed?

What test can you apply to a man? How do you judge an inner character? Every man is a thousand men, a short acquaintanceship is insufficient and a snap judgement is dangerous. The best test of Harrison Marks are his friends.

Obviously, he has an enormous circle of acquaintances; for this test, discount them. There is, however, a legion of real friends, always someone is dropping in at the St. John's Wood flat. And these friendships have lasted continuously for years. The models, the mistresses… the wives. People from widely diverse walks of life, for years and years the easy, intimate relationships have continued and deepened. It doesn't matter "whether they are loaded or haven't got a pot to piss in" they all have something to offer and Harrison Marks has a lot to give in the way of friendship — and it lasts, which is a good test of quality. And nearly all his girlfriends have remained very good friends with him.

So *au revoir*, London; hello, Hollywood. No matter how great the success, how sweet the life in the sun, it is doubtful if Hollywood will ever claim Harrison Marks permanently.

He is a Londoner. A supreme example of a Londoner: tough, resilient, full of fun, equally full of sentiment. The smog of that city courses through his veins. The grit and grime are ingrained in him. The smell and taste of the place are in his nostrils and mouth.

No matter how good it is elsewhere, like a salmon in the spawning season some compulsion will bring him back.

Part of that compulsion will be loyalty to the people who will be waiting at home for him.

People like Wynne, who has worked with him since 1954. "Twelve years or more in this madhouse and loving every minute of it, and still sane," she says.

"He made his will the other day and I told him, 'I'll bet the only thing you've left me is all the worries.' "

Once again the whole business burden will fall on her shoulders and still she'll quicken the morning with a bright smile. "You're getting old, Wynne," he says when she's pressing a point. "Twelve years with you and I feel like Methuselah," she replies. But she'll still knock up a plate of delicious spaghetti bolognaise in the studio if things are too rushed to go out to lunch.

And there is Tony Roberts, the man who arrived nine years ago purely to mend the sash cords and was so intrigued that he stayed until now, and became studio manager.

"One of my closest friends and really my right hand," says Harrison Marks. "The only person I trust entirely and completely and utterly professionally. And apart from that, we're almost brothers. The three of us have grown up together as a team and we've developed a terrific loyalty. Without these two I feel, well, naked — naked as nature intended."

What else did Vivienne teach? Loyalty, love, tolerance, a regard for other people?

Lucky Leo's, they always fall on their feet. Suddenly there was a second Toni, this one with an "i" — blonde hair and very attractive. A sweet, affectionate girl with an enormous capacity for understanding. The one person who has ever brought contentment into his life. And the one who has never tried to put him in chains.

"She is someone I love," he says simply, "and I do realise I do love her. She puts up with my lunatic ways and my day-dreams. She makes me happy, and I make her happy. Really, for the first time, I am as happy as an ordinary, average person. She is my anchor to a sane, normal contented life."

If there are any chains to be put on, Harrison Marks is putting them on to himself. "I love Toni," he says, "and I know that I mean it."

Hollywood: "The film we're going to shoot is like Mondo Cane', but much lighter and funnier. We've adapted it from a book by Carol Lindsey. This was a best-seller in America. All about the idiocies of people in California. You know, the Forest Lawns Cemetery, the dude ranches and lots of other queer affairs. People do the weirdest things. Basically, people are funny.

"I've got a feeling it's going to be great and I'm just the bloke to do it.

"The title? Didn't I tell you the title? Oh, it's very apposite. It's called, 'Climate of Lunacy!' "

www.ingramcontent.com/pod-product-compliance
Ingram Content Group UK Ltd.
Pitfield, Milton Keynes, MK11 3LW, UK
UKHW041955190726
13854UKWH00005B/1988

9 781999 744106